The Doctrine of God

Ronald Gregor Smith

The Doctrine of God

*Edited and prepared for
publication by K. Gregor Smith
and A. D. Galloway*

The Westminster Press
Philadelphia

ISBN 0–664–20889–4

Library of Congress Catalog Card No. 79–110726

Published by The Westminster Press ®
Philadelphia, Pennsylvania

Printed in the United States of America

Contents

To the Theological Faculty of the University of Marburg as a small token of gratitude for the conferring on the author of the degree of Doctor of Theology *honoris causa*

Editors' Foreword

At the time of his sudden and tragic death, Ronald Gregor Smith was engaged in preparation of the Warfield Lectures to be delivered at Princeton Theological Seminary this year. From the partially completed manuscript and notes which he left, this book has been reconstructed and is now being published as the Warfield Lectures for 1969. For the first four lectures a continuous text existed. Apart from the completion of a few references, these chapters are published as he left them. It is clear from his marginal notes that he intended to revise and re-write them before publication. But rather than come between him and his readers we have thought it best to publish the text of these lectures more or less as it stands. For the same reason we have tried to use only his own words in reconstructing the last two lectures from fragmentary notes. Apart from a few bridging sentences, the words in Lectures 5 and 6 are his. But the arrangement of them and the reconstruction of the argument is ours. Had Ronald Gregor Smith lived to complete it, this would have been a much better book. As it is, we must be thankful for what we have.

K.G.S.
A.D.G.

Introduction

Ronald Gregor Smith may well be the most important English-speaking theologian of this generation and this, I believe, is his most significant book.

He is of crucial importance for the contemporary development of theology because he had the gift of prophecy in a remarkable degree. A prophet is a man who sees what is available for everyone else to see; but he sees into it and through it and beyond it. Within the matrix of the present he can find the centre of creativity out of which the future will grow. So he can speak not only to his own day but of and to the day which is yet to come. It is in this sense that Ronald Gregor Smith was a prophetic writer.

As early as 1937, when he translated Martin Buber's *I and Thou*, he put his finger on a work which has provided the key concepts for one of the main lines of theological advance in this century. In 1956, when he published *The New Man*, he anticipated both the mood and the substance of the theological decade just passed, with its emphasis on life in this world and the renewal of that life, not by the naïve programmes of liberalism but

9

through a radical re-interpretation of Christian eschatology. He was the pathfinder of that movement in
theology which culminated in the *Honest to God* debate.[1]

Yet the name of Professor Gregor Smith was seldom
prominent in such popular theological debates. By the
time the debate had become extensive and popular he
was already looking over the horizon to the next stage.
One exception was the very public and regrettably heated
debate which took place in New Zealand and Australia.
It centred on some quite incidental remarks in Gregor
Smith's *Secular Christianity*.[2] This book, which he published in 1966, has not yet come into its own. It has
suffered, largely through the accident of its title, from
association with a brash and rather self-satisfied tendency
in much recent theology to find in contemporary
pluralist society an unambiguously appropriate medium
for the expression of Christian life and piety. Those
critics who attempted to associate him with the 'death of
God' theologians were singularly wide of the mark—just
how wide this present book will show. I believe that in
ten years' time we will read and value *Secular Christianity*
not merely for the daring novelty and intellectual
buoyancy of its interpretation of Christian doctrine but
as pointing the way to the theological foundations of the
movement which it anticipates. What is this movement?
It is the movement which is beginning to arise out of the
intense moral passion of our age. We are at the beginning

[1] As is acknowledged by John A. T. Robinson, *Honest to God*, SCM
Press, p. 26.
[2] See, for example, Lloyd Geering, *God in the New World*, Hodder and
Stoughton, London, 1968.

of an age which is coming to realize its absolute responsibility for the historic destiny of the peoples of the world. It has this responsibility in a new way because it now has the power to determine their history.

There is a movement of the spirit in response to this new age. It emerged clearly for the first time in the Fourth Assembly of the World Council of Churches at Uppsala in 1968. It is the spirit which will dominate the ethos of the World Church in the seventies. *Secular Christianity* has more in common with this determination to make human history a fully moral undertaking than it has with the surrealist probings of the 'death of God' theologians or the urbanity of contemporary secularism.

As well as having this sensitivity which enabled him to see a little farther than the rest of us, he had a knack also of seeing the dangers of excess in every movement. At the time when a shallow social gospel was dying a natural death he re-introduced depth and penetration into our conception of individual human existence through his work on Buber and Kierkegaard. But as soon as existentialism began to become a vogue he had already moved on and was thinking of the dangers of its individualism and its inward-looking attitudes. His work on Hamann (*J. G. Hamann, A Study in Christian Existence*, Collins, 1960) reflects his perception of the need for an existentialism which had a positive relation to the sweep of human history as well as to the moment of individual decision—which expressed the graciousness of the world as well as its infinite distance from God. Conversely, his selection of material from the later diaries of Kierkegaard (*The*

Last Years, Journals 1853-55, by Søren Kierkegaard, edited and translated by Ronald Gregor Smith, Collins, 1965) exposed not only the magnificent rigour of Kierkegaard's mind, but also the unwholesome isolation from the world, the Church and society to which it led him.

So we find in Ronald Gregor Smith a combination of two insights in lively tension with one another—on the one hand a penetrating perception of the significance of the individual person; on the other hand a sympathy with the whole of history, with all that it means to say that this world is God's world, that the history of this world is God's most intimate concern.

It was this Janus-faced wisdom, this two-sided vision of the truth that set Ronald Gregor Smith the problem of what tragically turned out to be his own last years— how to combine the piercing vision of Kierkegaard's concern for the authentic individuality of the single one with an honest and wholesome concern for the whole world as God's world and for all history as God's history. It is out of this tension that the present book is generated. How does God meet us in the worldliness of our world? What does it mean that some of us still feel compelled to talk of God even though we are immersed in the secularity of the world just as deeply as our neighbour who feels no need to talk about God at all?

This is a problem which has already received a good deal of attention from logicians and philosophers in this century. Gregor Smith was well aware of this. Yet he ignored most of what has been written on the subject not because he thought lightly of it, but because he knew that his own contribution was not to be made along those lines. His own contribution had to be spoken out of that point at which three lines of thought intersect—that of Kierkegaard with his uncompromising challenge to the individual; that of Martin Buber with his uncompromising recognition of the claims of the 'other' as the neighbour before whom the single one stands and from whom he receives his dignity as a person; and that of Dietrich Bonhoeffer for whom the world, the world of 'It' in which the individual and his neighbour meet, is God's world and the medium of God's presence. These are the three co-ordinates which determine the position which Gregor Smith here expounds.

The Free Man (Collins, 1969), which recapitulates some of his earlier work and also makes some advance, is an excellent bridge to and preparation for the present book.

There is no point in pretending that *The Doctrine of God* is an easy book. Despite all the simplicity and directness of Gregor Smith's style, the argument is difficult and complex. But it is worth the effort, and it will reward the effort of anyone who is prepared to try.

His choice of title is significant. At a time when everyone is seeking out titles which proclaim their indifference to traditional ways of speaking in theology, Ronald Gregor Smith resolutely chooses a title which declares his reverence for the traditional ways of speaking about God. His first chapter deals with the received doctrine of the Church. In these documents the history that produced us and made us what we are now rises up and confronts us. Gregor Smith, speaking out of his own situation, refers to the tradition which he himself has received—the tradition of the Church of Scotland and the *Westminster Confession of Faith*. But it is not of the *Westminster Confession* as such that he speaks but of that tradition which every man receives as his own tradition and out of which he builds his own specific identity. We need this nourishment from the past. Without it we would amount to nothing. Yet we fall short of the level of responsible, historical existence if we merely receive and repeat this tradition. We deal with it responsibly by responding to it in the novelty of our own situation. So our relation to the history out of which the tradition speaks to us is intimately bound up with our relation to God.

But today there is a special crisis about God. It is not just a conflict between different ideas of God. Rather, God is simply dropping out of the picture. The highly abstract God of metaphysical theology seems irrelevant. The concrete, personal God of biblical revelation seems incredible. How does one re-establish a love affair that has grown cold? Do we recover the reality of God by recovering the old idea of him? This will not do. Historic existence moves forward, never back, and it never stands still. You cannot fix the living God in a permanent, unchanging confession without turning him into a lifeless object. Yet a God who does not transcend the flux of history—who dances to the tune of every changing fashion of thought—is a mere aspect of history. This conflict has always been present in the tension between the changeless God of philosophical theology and the active God of biblical revelation. But today it has reached critical proportions.

The whole problem needs a fresh approach. This must be one in which reason and faith, the inner-worldly and the transcendent, are differently understood. They must not be so conceived that they are set in irreconcilable opposition from the outset.

Rational, philosophical theology has bequeathed to us the notion of God as 'Being'. (He can scarcely be 'a being'—one item beside others.) The biblical tradition also speaks of God in terms of 'Being'—especially in the divine name 'I am that I am'. But this apparent, easy agreement between the philosophical-metaphysical doctrine of God on the one hand and the biblical-revealed doctrine of God on the other only hides another aspect of the conflict within our idea of God. In this connection Gregor Smith's discussion and application of recent interpretations of the divine 'I am' of Exodus 3 : 14 is crucial for the argument. This 'I am' is fundamentally different from the 'Being' of classical metaphysics. It is the 'I am present', 'I shall be there' of one who comes actively as a presence within history.

History is the basic category of human existence. Other creatures exist in time, but only man has a history; and only the Christian faith unveils the essential structure of historical existence. Therefore, the only way we can come to a new understanding of the God who makes himself present in history is through a new and more penetrating understanding of man in his historicity.

But what do we mean by 'history'? Gregor Smith has

often been criticized for his failure to define this word on which he leans so heavily. But in this his critics misunderstand the manner of speech he is using. When he speaks of history he is in effect saying: 'Behold, I show you a mystery.' A mystery is not disclosed by precision of definition but by the communication of a vision.

Seen in terms of the vision of history illuminated by faith which Gregor Smith sets before us, transcendence is not something excluded from the sphere of the human, nor does it exclude the human. It is integral to the experience which distinguishes us as men. It is the experience of the world as something graciously given into our care. It is the experience of our neighbour as the 'other' who graciously gives us recognition as a person.

This is not any kind of reductionism. It is not and never has been Gregor Smith's intention to suggest that God is something less than our forefathers believed him to be. On the contrary, his intention is always to magnify the name of the Lord. He is not suggesting, after the manner of Feuerbach, that our meeting with God is 'only' our experience of the world and our neighbour. Our experience of being together with the other can be derived neither from the 'I' of self nor the 'Thou' of the other but only from what is *beyond* both.

But what is this 'beyond'? It is the Word, which is the basis of all communication and the Spirit, which is the basis of all communion. But it is in our worldly history, not apart from it, that God is known in his Word and Spirit. This is the history whose essential nature is disclosed in Jesus Christ and understood in faith. It is a form of being together in the world with others in such a way that 'where two or three are gathered together in his name, there is he in the midst of them'.

How far does this take us? I can do no better than quote the last sentences of Chapter 4:

'In what way are we to understand the Word as being related to the historical Jesus? In what way as identical with God? In what way as being the all-inclusive Spirit, identical with both Father and Son?

'I ask "in what way?" For the real question is not *what* Jesus is, or *what* the Spirit is, or *what* God the Father is; but the question is *how* we are to understand ourselves in relation to the realities indicated by these names. If we can begin to understand in what way we may accept our own history, we shall be on the way. And the Christian faith does not really propose more than a way for us to walk.'

But does this way not lead to sheer anthropomorphism —or to a theology in which God is simply buried within history? This is the central question of Chapter 5. It gives rise to a very important discussion of the 'death of God' theologies in which, despite his sympathetic understanding of their intention, the vast gulf which separates Gregor Smith from that line of thought becomes more apparent than in his earlier writing.

This is not in the least because he wished to retreat from the affirmation of Christian secularity in his earlier work. On the contrary, he thought it the malaise of modern secularity that it is not secular enough. It has become an ideology cutting loose from its own historic sources. It needs to rediscover its own roots in faith in the

God who frees man and his world to be themselves. Rightly understood thorough-going secularity does not deny but depends upon the transcendence of God.

Again and again, as I worked through the notes on which these last chapters are based, I came across the exclamation, 'Transcendence is what I must concentrate on!'

But this is a transcendence which cannot be disclosed in a mere pageant of ancient verbiage. It is to be found only as we make our own history in response to the history that has been given to us in Jesus Christ. It has to be recognized in a new perception of the reality of Word and Spirit within our daily commerce. From this perception we can begin to feel our way towards the new theological categories which we need to bring both Word and Spirit—and so the transcendence of God as it is disclosed in man—to clear expression.

The programme of work which Gregor Smith so hopefully sketched out for himself in his rough drafts of these last chapters has become our inheritance and our responsibility.

University of Glasgow   A. D. GALLOWAY
1 May 1969

'Do thou, O Lord my God, teach my heart where and how to seek thee, where and how to find thee. Lord, if thou art not here, where shall I seek thee who art absent? But if thou art everywhere, why do I not see thee who art present? But surely thou dwellest in "light inaccessible". And where is light inaccessible? Or how shall I approach light inaccessible? Or who will lead me and bring me into it, that I may see thee there? . . . I was made in order to see thee, and I have not yet done that for which I was made . . . I am not trying, O Lord, to penetrate thy loftiness, for I cannot begin to match my understanding with it, but I desire in some measure to understand thy truth, which my heart believes and loves. For I do not seek to understand in order to believe, but I believe in order to understand. For this too I believe, that "unless I believe, I shall not understand".' St Anselm, *Proslogion* I.

CHAPTER ONE

Faith and Doctrine

In choosing as the title of these lectures the traditional phrase 'the doctrine of God', I might seem to be missing the chance of being attractive. Would not some more fashionable phrase, such as 'God-language', or 'the death of God', or 'God up there' (of course with a question-mark), or 'God as the ground of being', or 'an atheist theology', be more likely to catch the imagination and seize the attention?

> I must confess that I have been tempted. Yet it seems to me that there is a certain lack of seriousness in many of the recent essays on the theme of God. This might seem an odd comment upon work which is often audacious, and pro-vocative, and written with a consuming passion or with an elegant coolness, in which the author's heart or his head—and sometimes both—is thoroughly engaged. How can they be described as lacking in seriousness? I mean that they lack the context of the tradition out of which their essays have come. And because this is so, they also lack the final mark of true seriousness: the ability to be witty, the touch of light-heartedness, the relaxation which is only possible within the sure and clear ambit of a long and arduously elaborated tradition.

However instructive the topical concern with the subject of God may be—and I hope to show how I have learned from it—what is chiefly now required, I believe, is a sustained effort to relate our particular modern problems to the laborious procedures of our predecessors: in a word, to the tradition indicated in the word 'doctrine'.

Does this simply mean that we can take refuge in objectifying discourse? Can we conveniently ignore everything else: our subjective stances, our fancies, our doubts, our fears for the future?—and by 'our' I mean those of us who have felt the immensities of the changes which are surging around and within us, breaking down old structures and calling everything in question: and does that not mean all of us? And further, does the recourse to our traditions mean that we can also conveniently ignore the pressures which, for the present, I can only loosely circumscribe as the existential pressures which come athwart our course under the name of God?

None of this can be ignored. We can neither omit the name of God, nor make free of it. The real audacity does not consist in declaring that God is dead, but in daring at all to take that name upon our lips.

Martin Buber tells a story, in the introduction to his book, *The Eclipse of God*, of how a friend had expostulated with him about his use of the name of God. The friend said:

'How can you bring yourself to say "God" time after time?... What you mean by the name of God is something above all human grasp and comprehension, but in speaking about it you have lowered it to human conceptualization. What word of human speech is so misused, so defiled, so desecrated as this! All the innocent blood that has been shed for it has robbed it of its radiance. All the injustice that it has been used to cover has effaced its features. When I hear the highest called "God", it sometimes seems almost blasphemous.'

To this criticism Buber replied:

'Yes, it is the most heavy-laden of all human words. None has become so soiled, so mutilated. Just for this reason I may not abandon it. Generations of men have laid the burden of their anxious lives upon this word, and weighed it to the ground; it lies in the dust and bears their whole burden. . . . Where might I find a word like to describe the highest! If I took the purest, most sparkling concept from the inner treasure-chamber of the philosophers, I could only capture thereby an unbinding product of thought. I could not capture the presence of Him whom the generations of men have honoured and degraded with their awesome living and dying. I do indeed mean Him whom the hell-tormented and heaven-storming generations of men mean. . . . But when all madness and delusion fall to dust, when they stand over against Him in the loneliest darkness and no longer say "He, He" but rather sigh "Thou", shout "Thou", all of them the one word, and when they add "God", is it not the real God whom they all implore, the One Living God, the God of the children of man ? . . . And just for this reason is not the word "God", the word of appeal, the word which has become a *name*, consecrated in all human tongues for all time ?'[1]

I wish later to examine both the strength and the weakness of Buber's philosophy of the Thou, with its

[1] Martin Buber, *Eclipse of God*, Harper, New York, 1952, and Gollancz, London, 1953, pp. 16 f.

valiant but not entirely convincing attempt to establish an ontology of personal relations.[1] Here I simply wish to draw from his words some of the strength of his sensibility and of his delicate imagination, in order to emphasize that there is more than one approach to inherited doctrine. 'A hearty personal faith in the system of doctrine'[2] which we have inherited from our Reformed tradition is not necessarily identical with a view of doctrine as playing a normative role in Christian theology. That is to say, we do not find ourselves obliged to hold that certain teachings provide for Christian faith its specific and definite and definitively formulated subject-matter. Neither the teaching as a whole, nor the way in which the teaching is to be understood, is prescribed for us in the genuine doctrinal tradition. The subject-matter of Christian faith is not a fixed deposit which can be historically ascertained, and which is then to be accepted in a way that is congruent with the traditional formula-

[1] See pp. 96 ff. and 126 ff.

[2] cf. the terms of the Warfield Trust. However, the framers of the *Westminster Confession*, and even more clearly the makers of the *Scots Confession* of 1560, were well aware of the provisional and even of the fragmentary nature of their formulations. In particular, the words in the preface of the *Scots Confession* are disarmingly revealing:

'Protestand that gif onie man will note in this our confession onie Artickle or sentence repugnand to Gods halie word, that it wald pleis him of his gentlenes and for christian charities sake to admonish us of the same in writing; and we upon our honoures and fidelitie, be Gods grace do promise unto him satisfactioun fra the mouth of God, that is fra his haly scriptures, or else reformation of that quhilk he sal prove to be amisse.' (In the edition of the Church of Scotland Committee on Publications, Edinburgh, 1937, p. 41.)

tions of the historical deposit. Faith is not a matter of historical research, with the implications that we have simply to discover what is lying there, re-think it on its own terms and then obey the claims which it embodies. This would be a parody of faith, and the ruin of the tradition.

It might, however, be urged that the procedure I have outlined is also a parody of the way even the most conservative theologian today would handle traditional doctrine. Certainly, it is true that the general problem of our present relation to historical documents requires considerable attention if we are to establish a reasonable position which can command a real consensus. For it is of great importance for the churches that there should be sufficient agreement to permit both liberal and conservative to understand one another in the love of a common allegiance. This can only be achieved, it seems to me, if the liberal can be acknowledged by the conservative to be also, in his way, conserving; and if the conservative likewise can be acknowledged by the liberal to be also, in his way, liberalizing. But certainly this does mean that the present positions of liberal and conservative are equally untenable.

If I may put in one sentence what I wish to assert in this opening lecture, it is that I regard doctrine as having a real but limited function in the life of Christian faith.

Certainly, without the willingness to think through the received documents of our tradition, I could not venture to stand before you now, or to account myself a reasonable heir not merely of the documents of the Reformed tradition, but also of the whole material of the Christian tradition. For the readiness to understand our past is the prime prerequisite for facing the future in a responsible way.

But this does not mean that there is a normative character adhering to the traditional doctrines. The reasonable demand that we should ascertain what in fact are the traditional doctrines, and then that we should think them through, does not carry with it the demand that we should simply obey the claims implicit in them. The obedience which is a classic element in the life of Christian faith is not identical with acceptance of certain propositions as true.

Rather, the question which faces us here, in this provisional exploration of the issues of faith and doctrine, is: What is the reality indicated in the credal and confessional statements of the tradition? More precisely still: Where and when is this reality? And, to put the question personally: How am I, how are you, related to such past events of the Christian tradition? Or, to enlarge the horizon, and put this personal question in the concrete form of human existence: How (in Kierkegaard's words) am I related to past events for my eternal salvation?

With this last formulation of the question I have made a significant shift of ground. For I am not now merely asking about the context and *Sitz im Leben* of particular systematic communications out of the past. But I am asking, What do these communications point to? Where are the events to which the communications of the tradition point?

I for my part am not implying that the assertions of the tradition are false. On the contrary, it is important to recognize that in their way they are true. But at the same time they are not the truth. At most we can say that in their way they point to the truth.

Something similar must be said of every historical communication. All that comes to us out of the past, the whole *traditum* of the tradition, the creeds, the confessions, the deliverances of councils and assemblies, but also the rituals and liturgies, the hymns and the prayers and the uncountable treatises, tractates, broadsheets, the hardbacks and the paperbacks, concerning the Christian tradition: all, without any doubt, have their place. But they are not the truth.

Even infinitesimally, they have their grain of truth. And even when their place is grand and assured, still it is only their few grains.

At best, each points, in its own way, to the truth. They do not, even under the most propitious circumstances, possess the truth.

Doubtless there would be general agreement among the broad groupings within the churches if I were to confine my judgment to the mass of transient religious writings, what Karl Rahner calls the three popular varieties, of *haute vulgarisation*, theological journalism and theological freebootery—adding to these what he calls the 'often necessary and sometimes superfluous writings in which the mass of the faithful needs to have the daily bread of its religious instruction new baked, new every day, even if it looks the same today as it did yesterday.'[1]

But if I suggest, as I do, that it is the whole tradition which is here under survey and judgment, then I am not so sure that a parting of the ways is not already reached. For of course included in the whole tradition is Scripture itself. Scripture too must be understood not as itself being the truth, but as pointing, in its own manifold ways (corresponding to the manifold nature of Scripture), to the truth.

It might at once be objected that if we relinquish the normative status of all tradition, both written and unwritten, then it might look as though we were launched on a sea without limits, where there are no landmarks to guide us and no harbour awaiting us. And of such documents as the *Westminster Confession*, whatever their effects upon faith and whatever the ways in which they have been manipulated for the sake of an alleged norm of faith, at least we can say that they have been deliberately and firmly anchored on the rock of Scripture.

And the intention of this is easy to appreciate. Without a firm and solid grip on the past out of which we have come, there can be no order, no clear line, and thus no future. And the written documents of Scripture do at least offer a solid grip. On closer inspection, however, and by inescapable modern standards of literary and

[1] Karl Rahner, *Theological Investigations*, Vol. I, Darton, Longman and Todd, London, 1961, p. 1.

historical criticism, the order and the clear line of Scripture are not so manifestly indisputable as the formulators of theories about Scripture once thought.

The principle of understanding which is implicit in the empirical and venerable procedure and style of all creeds and confessions, and in the formulation of the written tradition of Scripture itself, needs to be more closely investigated, if it is to be regarded as anything more than a formal gesture indicating the positive historical actualities which are alleged to be at the heart of the Christian tradition.

I say 'alleged' to be there, not because I wish to adopt a position of scepticism regarding the historical reality which is both the source and the style of a living Christian faith; but because I am unable to take my starting-point from what seems to me to be an extremely sceptical assumption of a dichotomy between the so-called historical 'actualities' or 'facts' of the past (the historical *traditum*) on the one hand, and the appropriation of this tradition by means of faith. The issue here is by no means simple, and a premature foreclosing of the issue is able to lead to all kinds of unfortunate misunderstandings.

The underlying difficulty is not easy to express. Even to attempt to express it involves us in the suspicion of *parti pris*. For I should like to suggest that in the formulation of confessions, and even in the formulation of the scriptural tradition, a certain positivism, even a fundamentalist positivism, is inevitably connected. I am not thinking here of the baser sorts of literalism, with their unhappy reliance upon a pre-Enlightenment understanding of literary and historical criticism, but rather of a more deep-seated fundamentalism which has been termed 'cultural fundamentalism'.[1] This involves a reliance upon the 'given' of communications which claim, in one way or the other, to be the authoritative truth. The line between this reliance and a static view of the truth is very narrow. Indeed, in practice there is no distinction. For a reliance of this kind aims at preserving the past on its own terms. It is therefore assumed as beyond discussion that the given formulation of past events in terms of specific propositions is true. Revolution, change, novelty, newness are *a priori* suspect. The future is therefore mortgaged by the expenses of the past. So it is assumed that the only way for faith to operate is that it should re-enter the world of the Bible, or the thought-world of some chosen span of the tradition, whether canonical or extra-canonical, and thus re-establish the truth as it was once and once for all delivered to the saints.

The basic question here, which lies behind various differences about the place of tradition and of Scripture in determining faith, is the question of hermeneutics. The centuries of controversy between Protestant and Roman Catholic theologians on these matters have ended in a strange lull, and shifting of fronts. For it is now seen— at least by those on both sides who are not gorged on a surfeit of doctrine—that it is the way in which we

[1] I first came upon this phrase in an article on 'Ethical Problems of Contemporary Society' by Robert Lee in *A Dictionary of Christian Ethics*, ed. J. Macquarrie, SCM Press, London, 1967, *ad loc.*, p. 71.

understand that determines both our approach and our conclusion. This way of understanding is by no means simple. Primarily, it means the way in which we understand ourselves in relation to the past. Clearly this is bound to involve the present. We have to understand from where we are: we cannot do anything else. But this present situation of ours is not as it were an empty vessel waiting to be filled with the findings of the past. It is not even a vessel filled with impurities, false views and prejudices and rebellious disinclination to hear the words coming from out of the past. Rather, this present situation is, for each one of us, one in which we are already embedded—but in our own way, in the way peculiar to our own time and circumstances—in the structures of tradition.

The heart of this situation is the language we use. Language is the concrete sign of our historicity. At the same time it is the clear defiance of any interpretation of our present situation as being dominated by subjectivism. The common charge levelled against any hermeneutical position which appears to deviate from what I have called fundamentalist positivism, or a theory of normative truths established in the past, is that it dissolves everything in a subjectivist mist, that it is cavalier in its treatment of historical facts and that, in general, it depends more upon 'spiritual experiences' than upon the severe objectivity of what has happened, and what can be proved and demonstrated to have happened. But language expresses our understanding of the past in terms of a present event, which is not a subjective or private or interior experience merely (though, of course, private and interior experience is not excluded) but is a public event. This is what I understand Dr Ernst Fuchs to mean by a 'speech-event'. Modern hermeneutics is the unity, in language, of past events with present decisions. Thus I do not, in the process of understanding, simply conceptualize the past: but I respond to the truth which I meet in each new hermeneutical situation. This responding to the truth is a *doing* the truth. Truth is more than concepts. Exegesis therefore means, as Fuchs says, 'standing in the event'. Exegesis is not just 'a reflective relation to an event which is there without that relation'.[1]

Or, if we may quote J. G. Hamann, whose whole theological and philosophical position was an early and unjustifiably neglected struggle to reach an adequate hermeneutic: 'The field of history has always appeared to me to be like that wide field that was full of bones, and behold they were very dry. Only a prophet can prophesy of these bones, that veins and flesh will grow on them and skin cover them. They have still no breath in them, till the prophet prophesies.'[2]

To put it another way, the question of hermeneutics is the question of temporality. More specifically, it is the question of our involvement in time. This everyday particularity of our human experience can clearly not be determined out of hand. Nevertheless, for our purposes a few elementary considerations can be presented. Our

[1] Carl Michalson, *Worldly Theology*, Scribner's, New York, 1967, p. 108.
[2] *Sämtliche Werke*, ed. J. Nadler, Herder, Vienna, 1951, Vol. III, p. 398. cf. R. Gregor Smith, *J. G. Hamann: A Study in Christian Existence*, Collins, 1960, p. 91.

temporality includes the future as well as the past. For the Christian tradition in particular this means that we are involved at the same time (that is, at this same present time) in a relation to the past and a relation to the future. The Christian tradition runs backwards and forwards along the time scale. What we are now is shaped by the way we accept the past. But the whole complex of acceptance and refusal, of choice and decision, of trembling and of aversion, is also shaped by the way we face the future. Fear and hope are the warring partners in this forward look. But this is not to say that subjectivity dominates the interpretation in such a way that it ends by being a mere psychological subjectivism. Fear and hope are inadequately described as merely inward psychic states. Rather, in the context of temporality they point to an ontology which is a historical reality. For the issue of the struggle between fear and hope decides whether we go forward in freedom and responsibility, with hope, or accept scepticism, with fear, as our norm for human existence.

Fear and hope are also involved in our relation to the past, that is, to the past as belonging to each one of us in its particular way. Here, too, an ontology arising out of scrutiny of the human condition can be elaborated. We shall have to go into this more fully when we face (in Lectures 5 and 6) the question of the historicity of God.

'The past can only be preserved in its purity by some-one who accepts responsibility for the future, who preserves in so far as he overcomes'.[1] We may agree with Rahner that it is the peculiarity of Christianity that it is not simply concerned with the reference to its origins. Does this mean that hermeneutics for a Christian understanding is different from secular hermeneutics? Not at all: to attempt to make a fundamental cleavage between 'secular' and Christian or 'sacred' hermeneutics would be a separation of spheres which in the end would lead to the destruction of both spheres. This would be of course primarily and most dramatically obvious with the Christian sphere. For a Christianity which was understood as having its own concerns, its own autonomous sphere, its own life and its own goal, separated from the concerns and life of all other historical traditions, would be a contradiction of the very heart and essence of the Christian understanding of reality. Nothing less than what is ultimately real is at stake here; and the reality of the Christian faith stands or falls with the reality of the ordinary historical world.

When we say that Christianity is not simply concerned with the reference to its origins, we mean that more than any other human historical phenomenon Christianity has shown itself again and again to be an extremely dynamic movement. That is to say, the constant reference back to the origins, and that means, of course, to the whole tradition, produces the reference to the future. The end is contained in the beginning. The forward look arises out of the backward glance. We cannot hope and pray for the coming kingdom unless it is already given to us

[1] Karl Rahner, *Theological Investigations*, Vol. I, p. 7.

in the beginning. But neither can we accept what is given to us in the beginning without finding ourselves hoping and praying for the coming.[1]

The extraordinary concentration of past and future in the Christian present is therefore something more than a theory of the world: for it is the way in which Christian faith understands and confesses that God speaks. The world in which we live, in Christian faith, is not a closed system. It is part of an irreversible historical movement. This is expressed, symbolically, in the form of faith 'listening' to God's speech. God's speech with man is an event which is full of promise. It is literally a promise, the word of promise.

Thus the norm cannot be systematized. Christ as the word of promise in person is the norm, the only norm, the *norma non normanda*, and this determines our understanding of Scripture and of the whole tradition. Only in this sense do the Reformers' words, *sola scriptura*, bear the whole weight of faith. Faith lives by Scripture so far as that means by the substance, the content, the principle of Scripture, which is Christ.

To sum up what I have so far said, God's speech with man is a happening, and the tradition has to struggle

---

[1] This is the perpetual significance of the symbol of the second coming. This is more than the mythological expression of a pious hope. It is the imaginative symbol for the dynamic historicity of Christian faith. Jürgen Moltmann, in his *Theology of Hope*, has done us all a service to lift us above historical and pseudo-historical considerations to a consideration of the renovating reality of hope—even though he has done this by a somewhat primitive depiction of eschatological reality in terms of past apocalyptic imaginings.

all the time with the down-to-earthness of this happening.

There is in our time, as has often been observed, a remarkable dissolution of hard frontiers, in particular those which have so long stood between the Protestant and the Roman Catholic views of Scripture and tradition. Today we may even note an odd and rather confusing tendency on the part of certain Catholic writers to take up the claim *sola scriptura* at the same time as some Protestant theologians are writing it off as obsolete. (Gerhard Ebeling's essay on '*Sola Scriptura* and Tradition' in his book *The Word of God and Tradition*, Collins, London, 1968, deals with this matter in a most stimulating manner.) There can be no doubt about the hopefulness of this dissolution of frontiers, so far as future ecumenical conversation is concerned. But our hopes cannot be fulfilled merely by a change of positions—the Catholic interpretation of tradition making use of *sola scriptura* in order simply to re-assert the priority of tradition itself over all other elements which might claim the authority to criticize tradition; and the Protestant acceptance of tradition in such a way that the written word of Scripture is now regarded as tradition, yet still as having an independent or autonomous reality for faith.

Rather, *sola scriptura* must be understood as the Reformers themselves understood it—as pointing to the living Word of God. This living Word of God, which is Jesus Christ as the norm, by no means eliminates the tradition, that is, the transmission both in oral and written tradition and in the persons of living witnessing believers. On the contrary, so intimate is the connection between Christ the living Word of God and the tradition of faith that it is possible, indeed it is necessary, to understand the coming of that living Word of God in terms of the faithful hearing and acceptance of the gospel as presented through the written words of Scripture.

We may summarize this intricate relationship between faith and doctrine, between Scripture and tradition, between man and Christ, by saying that it is primarily in the spoken word, in the word addressed to me in my situation, that faith arises. At the same time, the historical powers and the fundamental freedom of that word oblige us to reckon with the coming of that word in many different ways. The 'speaking' of a word, when it is recognized in faith as God's 'speech', can clearly not be limited by any barricades or guaranteed by any structures which are set up by men. If there were such a limitation, or such a claim to guarantee the coming of the Word, what in fact we would have would be the most sterile imaginable form of a law, destroying the free life of the Word through the changing possibilities of man's history. That this has often enough happened in the life of the Church cannot be denied. To recognize the fact is in itself some safeguard against the repetition of the act.

The tradition, then, and in particular the doctrinal tradition, is truly itself only when it throws itself away. That is, it is not the last word, just as it is not the first word. It is only within the dynamism of history as the place and the time of irreversible personal decisions that the Word is truly heard, and faith is truly active.

That the course of our reflections so far is not merely theoretical is illustrated by certain confused stirrings within the churches today. In general, it might perhaps be regarded as a hopeful sign that there is a certain recrudescence of interest in theology—or, to put it less

pretentiously, in understanding what faith is all about—
among the mass of the faithful. More significantly, there
is a certain interest among those who look on with a
certain wonder at the pretensions, and still more at the
performance, of professed believers. Unfortunately, however, there are also signs that this fresh interest is leading
to a hardening of fronts, to a digging-in in defence of
established positions, and altogether to the erection of
barriers against the threat of novelty.

This sharpening of the issues is running along different
lines from the old denominational cleavages. But it
would be a tragic outcome of the present shifting of
fronts if, instead of the old denominations, we were to
have a separation between the liberals and the con-
servatives, or between the academics and the 'people', or
however the split might come to be described.

It is true that heresy-hunts of the old style cannot easily
be engaged upon in a pluralist society such as ours. In
this respect, at least, the secularizing of the products of
faith, joined with the other, Greek tradition of a love of
discussion and a desire to persuade rather than to compel,
has established, however precariously, a certain space for
freedom. At the heart of all freedom, as its positive core,
is the freedom to believe. To maintain this freedom, for
oneself and for the other, demands the utmost vigour and
compassion. In practice, the dangers of cleavages, especially between those who desire a normative system of
doctrine and those who desire freedom at all costs, are
very great. One need only think of the passion behind a
movement like 'Kein anderes Evangelium' among Pro-

testants in Germany, or of the virulence with which a professor of theology in New Zealand was recently attacked by the self-styled 'New Zealand Association of Presbyterian Laymen', to see the danger signals.[1]

> This is, of course, merely a modern version of an old story. For our present purpose one of the more illuminating episodes in Scottish Church history concerned the trial and deposition of a young minister, John McLeod Campbell, for heretical views on the atonement. The core of the accusation levelled at him was not that he contradicted the teachings of the New Testament, but that his views were out of step with the teachings of the *Westminster Confession*. There was no doubt in the minds of his opponents that the teachings of the *Westminster Confession* were at this point absolutely determinative of good faith.

There is real tragedy here. I am not thinking simply of the personal fate of an individual who speaks in true responsible freedom, for in fact for such a man there are other consolations, implicit in that very power for which he pleads. But I am thinking of the tragedy inherent in all temporality. It is not enough to say that we do not do things like that nowadays, or to point proudly to the Declaratory Acts and similar codicils to our credal standards. For again and again the temptation inherent in the evanescence of all things bowls us over: we want

[1] Professor Lloyd Geering was the object of the attacks. He has recently published an account of his views in *God in the New World* (Hodder and Stoughton, London, 1968). Professor Ernst Käsemann's *Der Ruf der Freiheit* (Mohr, Tübingen, 1968) is a vigorous manifesto for the freedom of the Christian. [The latter work is now available in English as *Jesus Means Freedom* (SCM Press, 1969)—Ed.]

to fix things, we want to give them permanence. There are many ways in which this has been attempted. Above all, we must look back in admiration upon the stupendous effort made by Plato to establish the real world as consisting in the realm of ideas or 'forms', in which our transient realm of 'appearances' is enabled to participate, thus having a share in reality. But the tragedy lies in the fact that, even in Plato's thought, the more intense and comprehensive the effort to reach absoluteness, the more elusive becomes the reality which can be understood to be attached to the passing and relative world of time.

In the Christian tradition the tragedy is presented in an acute form. For here we have a message about man and the world and God which comes in the form of historical events. Even if we say that this message, or *kerygma*, is to be heard only in and through the tradition (and in 'tradition' I include, though in a special sense, the Scriptures), and that we cannot penetrate to the historical events themselves—and this is my own view, though elsewhere[1] I have suggested an understanding of history which can repel the charge of mere scepticism about the historical 'facts'—nevertheless, on any rational interpretation the Christian message is clearly not a fiction, not just an artist's story, but it is grounded in certain particular, admittedly mysterious rather than simple, events in the history of Israel. In accordance with the nature of all historical events those particular events, too, are relative, localized, particular and thoroughly temporal. The point

[1] In *Secular Christianity*, Collins, London, 1966, and Harper and Row, New York, 1967; *especially* pp. 101 ff.

of the tragedy is that the more successful the believing hearers of the tradition are, the more, that is to say, they formulate—whether in creeds or confessions, liturgies or songs or the shapes of buildings, or in any other of the innumerable social, artistic and political structures which have arisen within the tradition—certain specific claims to permanence, the more they tend to eliminate that very historicity, particularity and temporality which are essential to the message they wish to proclaim. For the kerygma is by nature dynamic: it tears down and sweeps away, it reduces our baggage allowance with quite ineffable unconcern. And it is open to the future and takes unpredictable forms in each changing situation. So it can neither be finalized nor absolutized. It is of the paradoxical nature of the Christian tradition that it is handed down from person to person, from generation to generation, from one social form and structure to another, in the free power of the Spirit. Everything has to begin again, with each person, each generation, each social structure.

It is a special irony, a tragic irony, that Lessing should have come into such an irreconcilable conflict with Hauptpastor Goeze of Hamburg. Lessing saw with unexcelled clarity the necessity in Christianity to refuse to be identified with a static and normative theological establishment. At the same time Pastor Goeze saw with equal clarity that Christian truth did not consist of 'eternal verities' in the sense of what Lessing called 'eternal truths of reason'. The truth of Christianity was out-and-out and through-and-through contingent. What hope of reconciliation between the two positions was possible? Lessing, who at least saw things more clearly, knew that he could not take the leap across that '*garstige Graben*', that ugly ditch, which only faith was capable of. Kierkegaard saw both sides, and took the leap, and has therefore established himself for ever as the knight of faith.

Of course this does not mean that there is no tradition, no stability or enduring power. It does not mean that everything is at the mercy of subjective whimsy. But it means that the tradition can only be truly itself when it is constantly being rescued from its own trend towards self-destruction. The tradition is always in danger, in danger of absolutizing itself. And this is the negation of the freedom of the Spirit, which gave rise to the tradition.

If the objection is raised that nevertheless we cannot dispense with a firm rule of faith, I reply that the view of the tradition of the Christian kerygma which I am suggesting here is directed precisely towards establishing the reality of the kerygma. And basically this reality concerns the freedom of the Spirit. Can this freedom be expressed in the form of a rule of faith at all?

The classic and tragic protagonist of Christian freedom is Tertullian. At the same time he is the exponent and rigid adherent of the rule of faith. He ended in the wilderness. Even the excesses of Montanism did not satisfy him. Or perhaps it is fairer to say that the excesses of Montanism drove him into an ever more passionate search for a solution to the tragic ambivalence of Christianity, which he was never able to find. The resemblance between the style and the fate of Tertullian and that of Kierkegaard has often been remarked upon.

We must reply that the power of the freedom of the Spirit is not an arbitrary matter. The eschatological reality which is present as the gift of the kerygma gives form and coherence to the free movement of the Spirit. To put this in simpler though more ambiguous terms, because the Christian message is about God in Christ, we are not simply left to our own devices when it comes to handling the tradition. But we are offered the reality of a life which is taken out of the old, apparently endless, search for a reality beyond this temporal world. The magic of Plato is exorcised. We are offered the reality of a life which is at once here and now, without reservation, and also related both to the past through the whole kerygmatic tradition and also to the future, now seen as God's future.

This is the complex situation in which the eschatological reality of Christ is believed, and thus confirmed, in each new situation.

The conflict between Lessing and Hauptpastor Goeze was a struggle on the wrong terrain. The concepts of relative and absolute, when seen in the light of the ever new, ever freshly present kerygma, this message addressed to us in our particularity, here and now, do not have the effective power that is claimed for them by those classic antagonists. Far less can the modern proponents of a normative theology claim to have pinned down the absolute in their particular formulations.

Of course, my situation is relative in the sense that it is my own, and nobody else's, and that I have my own perspective on the whole tradition. And of course my hearing of the message addressed to me lifts me out of myself and puts me in a new perspective. Yet even this being lifted out of myself does not give me access to the absolute. For even if in some sense I can say that my life has been, or merely can be, completely changed by the Christian message, still, it is my life and my faith which are embodied in the changed situation. I am still myself, even if I can say, may dare to say, that it is no longer I but Christ that dwells in me.

But to say this is a very different thing from claiming that the relative has been absolutized, and that static forms can be established which provide the standard or norm of faith. The whole air is different. There we are in the realm of claim and counter-claim, of a uniform system of right thinking as the test, and, more, as the very substance, of faith. Faith in this realm is regarded as a set of propositions to be accepted by an act of willing obedience. But here in the realm of faith we live with other powers: here is the movement of the Spirit, faith as a risk and a gift, courage to persist and to hope, the joy of the Presence, and countless other gifts.

Is there complete incompatibility here? Must the tradition always produce forms, structures, claims, which tend to absolutize themselves? And must the assertion of the freedom of the Spirit, with all that this implies of a freely accepted and hearty and joyful conviction of faith, lead to formlessness, instability, enthusiasm, pietism, and finally to the wilderness where Tertullian and Kierke-gaard found themselves, alone? If the tradition, which was originally established as the expression of the historical gift of the Spirit, ends by quenching the Spirit, are we to say that on the other hand the claim to be free of absolute adherence to the fixed forms of the tradition leads to hopeless individualism and mere self-delusion?

If this clash between the Spirit and the historical products of the Spirit is indeed the last word, if it is both inevitable and insoluble, then the only possible outcome is scepticism. One way or the other we should have to accept the situation, and we could take our choice. Either we could accept a thoroughgoing empirical authoritarianism of tradition (whether that of the Bible or of the Pope would be, sociologically and psychologically speaking, of little moment), and by doing so would tacitly acknowledge that the reality of the Spirit is inaccessible. Or we could live in the wilderness, in the expectation of the coming of the Spirit, but without any hope that the coming would have anything to say or to do in the world of immutable traditions—like a John the Baptist without any realized eschatology. The first alternative is sceptical about the possibility of any newness in the world, whether coming from outside or from inside the received traditions. The second alternative is sceptical about the power of the Spirit really to participate in the destiny of man.

The question which faces us here might be put in less dramatic style if we ask ourselves whether conscious individual reflection can ever be institutionalized. Or more simply still, we can ask ourselves who the master is in the house of faith. The very nature of faith provides the answer. It is the nature of faith to be supremely personal and self-conscious; but at the same time conscious of its source, of its history and of its goal. Everything that comes to us out of the tradition must come under the scrutiny of the responsible, free and faithful enquiring mind. The understanding of what faith is, is the prime business of a living theology. Faith itself demands radical criticism of the tradition. So nothing in the tradition is the master, but everything is the servant of faith. And faith in turn is a gift, *the* gift, of the Spirit. Blind obedience to the tradition as it has again and again regarded itself is in truth the betrayal of what the tradition at its best has known and acknowledged that it stands for: namely, the provisional, often makeshift, and always insufficient witness to the reality of faith.

We may again quote Karl Rahner to provide a lapidary summary of the tensions which I have been describing. 'All human statements, even those in which faith expresses God's saving truths, are finite.'[1]

Of course, nothing of what has been said means the elimination of doctrine. Without the teaching that comes afresh to each generation there would be no stability or order or hope of permanence. But the stability and order and permanence dare never become isolated from the reality of faith as the ever new relationship to the kerygmatic reality.

This reality is an event, a happening: it is indeed the reality of Jesus Christ as the only norm. But it meets us in and through the whole mass of the tradition, including especially the communication of the tradition. This

[1] Karl Rahner, *Theological Investigations*, Vol. I, p. 43.

tradition includes the acknowledgment of the need for an active response of faith. This does not, however, turn the tradition into a private revelation or an opinion: the tradition remains primarily and essentially a public matter. The forms of its public communication are not restricted to credal or doctrinal propositions, however. They come in the manifold styles which have been elaborated by the human imagination, by artistic and constructive powers, as well as through reflection. The Christian tradition is a much more many-sided thing, more mysterious, more complex and splendid, more potent, than the over-intellectualized element in the tradition tends to assume.

Nevertheless, it is a fact that the communications of the tradition—the documents and the monuments, the rituals and liturgies and creeds and confessions—do bear the marks of objectivity: they are public and visible forms and structures. If they were not, they would not be able to be communications. The reality of the Spirit, calling us to newness, must not be construed as a denial of the past or of the necessary place of doctrine.

My purpose, so far, is satisfied, if I have been able to draw attention to the ever pressing tension between the forms of the past and the lively and disturbing reality of a present faith. Faith demands to be understood. And as soon as this demand is honestly faced, the traditional doctrines play their part: not as normative, not as a substitute for faith, but as servants in the house of faith. Faith without doctrine is a wildly swaying weathercock, driven around by every gust of the arbitrary imaginative or speculative power of men. Doctrine without faith is a sullen and joyless taskmaster, the slave-driver with the whip. There is no immutable doctrine; but the reality of the doctrinal tradition keeps faith from fantasy. The two must go together; but the greater of the two is faith.

CHAPTER TWO

The Crisis about God

I have spoken of the reality of faith as an event and have said that it entails, by its very nature, radical criticism of the tradition. This is the more clearly necessary in so far as the tradition again and again tends to solidify, as it were, and to become impervious to the very freedom and openness which are its *raison d'être*. Even the very core of the tradition, that is, the kerygmatic tradition, what has been handed down concerning God's message of the forgiveness and reconciliation of men through Christ, continually comes up against the desire in men to possess this message as a means of permanent security.

Thus we have the peculiar irony of a situation in which everything depends on man seeing that he is hopeless, and helpless of himself to secure himself in any ultimate sense, being transformed by man into a situation in which the reverse is attempted: out of a situation which is marked, humanly speaking, by complete insecurity and only divinely speaking, that is, in terms of the grace of forgiveness and reconciliation given by God to man, is marked by security, man attempts to turn the tables on God. Man wants to show that after all, even when it is a matter of grace, he can somehow exploit it for his own private advantage. The judgment which, as Adolf Schlatter so emphatically pointed out, does not precede grace but is the way in which grace operates,[1] in fact renders void man's efforts to manipulate grace.

Nevertheless, the gospel is in this way continually threatened with a new legalism. Even those who have once heard, and accepted in faith, the message of freedom and the way of openness are tempted to substitute for faith, received in the present word of promise, a new law which desires to win the mastery over time, and especially over the future. Sometimes, indeed, it seems as though the gift of openness to the future, recognized as God's future, were too great a reality for men to endure.

Perhaps the total invitation to forgiveness, acceptance and reconciliation needs to be understood much less in individualist terms and much more in corporate and relational terms. And the gift will then tend to be seen less as a kind of insurance policy with bonuses for the bourgeois individual, and more as the re-establishment of a mighty and unique community, the all-inclusive community centred upon God with man.

The great problem, therefore, is to incorporate in the present reality of faith the findings of the past in such a way that the future is not compromised by a wrong relation to the past. This is the problem of the right understanding of the experience which has been set down in the traditional forms, and especially in the teachings

[1] Quoted in Ernst Käsemann, *Der Ruf der Freiheit*, p. 40.

which have accumulated round the basic tradition of the kerygma concerning Christ.

This understanding, because it is the understanding which is sought by faith of its own source and significance, cannot permit the traditional teachings at any point to arrogate to themselves a position of final authority. Faith remains the master of the traditions. It can permit no absolute claim except the one which it has already heartily and joyfully accepted in the acceptance or forgiveness and the hope of renewal through God's active dealing with men in the kerygma concerning Christ. Yet at the same time faith's present acknowledgment of the Spirit is formed and shaped by its historical rootedness in the tradition which has as a matter of historical fact provided the structures for a continuing historical possibility. But this tradition has to be seen as making sense only in so far as it keeps open this possibility of the ever new happening of faith.

If this analysis of the complex relationships of faith and tradition is on the right lines, then we may hope that the doctrine of God may be capable of similar analysis. And as the doctrine of God, or more precisely belief in God, is properly regarded as the central doctrine in the whole tradition, so it is not surprising that precisely here the traditional structures of belief are questioned with the greatest vigour, and passion, and pathos.

My argument in the present lecture will be that faith's own self-understanding does not permit the straight-forward acceptance of the traditional formulation of the doctrine of God. It permits it neither as a normative doctrine, nor as carrying conviction in itself. The traditional doctrine of God has reached a dead end. But the crisis is about God, not just about a particular doctrine concerning God. Of course a concept formulated to express a conviction can become unreal, and unconvincing, without the necessary disappearance of the original conviction. Only the conviction must always find expression somehow—not necessarily in a satisfactory conceptual form. In the long run, however, an unidea'd conviction is sterile. Ideas give shape to even the simplest of faiths, and if the ideas are lacking, the faith, too, will wither.

The crisis about God today, therefore, if it really points to the end of the traditional doctrine, demands that a fresh start will have to be made. What that fresh start involves will be the matter for my subsequent lectures. Meantime, we must take a closer look at the nature of the impasse we have reached. We can conveniently do this by examining what the *Westminster Confession of Faith* has to say about the doctrine of God. In this way we shall have before us a characteristic example of what has passed, almost up to the present day, as the way in which God has to be understood and expressed.

But before we do this, we must recognize that the modern impasse in our thought about God is not an isolated intellectual problem for philosophers and theologians. It is part of a crisis in the Christian tradition which, so far as I know, is of unprecedented gravity. I shall not labour the details of this point at the moment. I wish simply to indicate the general and pervasive state of affairs. It is not so much in the explicit affirmations or negations of many philosophers and theologians—some of which will concern us in detail later—as in the tacit assumptions, in the whole style of contemporary society, that we are, I think, bound to recognize that God has simply dropped out of the picture. Not merely an idea of God, but the conviction of God's reality, is no longer operative in Western society as a whole.

Do we recover the reality of God by recovering the old idea of God? Or by furnishing a new idea of God? Or by re-entering the state of passionate conviction about God? How does one re-establish a love affair which has grown cold?

Before we can begin even to approach an answer to such questions, we must recognize the need for two concurrent activities: first, we must be ready to work at the historical problems connected with the formulation of doctrine. It is not without reason that Karl Barth spoke of the '*Unkultur*' (lack of culture) of the so-called death-of-God theologians. This was not a stricture upon their education or their theological sophistication, as I understand it, so much as a suggestion that they were not taking their own historical involvement in the Christian tradition seriously enough. In a sense, one might say, they were being too deadly serious about their own immediate situation.

The other activity which is required of us is precisely that which led to Barth's comment: it is the need for more passion.

The historical involvement is able to give us the long

perspective, when we can begin to realize, or at least to hope, that we have not reached the end of the story of God among men. The passionate involvement can lead us to realize, or at least to hope, that there is a way of understanding God which rests upon a more immediate confrontation than the traditional theological and philosophical categories have allowed. In this context the insights of artists and poets are without any doubt able to express the inarticulate experiences of the rest of us in such a way that conviction finds new forms and an old love lives again.

At the present time in Western history, however, it may be bluntly recorded that the way in which people generally live, plan their lives and express their deepest desires, simply leaves God out. The differences between the modern theologians who dispute whether God is to be regarded as missing, or absent, or hidden, or in eclipse, or dead, pale into insignificance beside this basic underlying assumption of our time, which sometimes looks as solid and immovable as a fact of nature, that God has ceased to be an active and powerful Name.

The traditional doctrine of God is set forth in solemn and splendid sentences in Chapter Two of the *Westminster Confession of Faith*. The first paragraph is as follows:

'There is but one only living and true God, who is infinite in being and perfection, a most pure spirit, invisible, without body, parts, or passions, immutable, immense, eternal, incomprehensible, almighty, most wise, most holy, most free, most absolute, working all things according to the counsel of his own immutable and most righteous will, for his own glory; most loving, gracious, merciful, long-suffering, abundant in goodness and truth, forgiving iniquity, transgression and sin; the rewarder of them that diligently seek him; and withal most just and terrible in his judgments; hating all sin, and who will by no means clear the guilty.'

Now it is not possible to take up each item of this description separately. Nor, indeed, is it necessary for our present purpose. What I wish to note here is that while the whole paragraph is supported by various references to Scripture, in fact twenty-four in all, the story behind each item, or the cash-value of each part of the description, is by no means uniform. The first group—down to the words 'for his own glory'—represents a combination of the procedures of the *via negativa*, the *via eminentiae* and the *via causalitatis*: that is, privative descriptions of what God is *not*, affirmative descriptions of God as possessing certain attributes in a supreme fashion ('most wise, most holy . . .'), and causal descriptions, which affirm certain contingent connections between the world and God's will. (The special significance of the words 'most absolute', with the accompanying Scripture reference to Exodus 3: 14, will have to be given detailed consideration when we come to consider the question of 'God as Being'.)[1]

In the second part of the paragraph we are introduced to what can only be described as totally and fundamentally different from the context of the first group. Here we are moving in a different realm of discourse. Descriptions like 'most loving, gracious, merciful', and so on, are

[1] See Chapter 3—especially pp. 93 ff.

connected with the anthropomorphic personalism which is so characteristic a *motif* in the biblical view of God.

But we must be careful here not to make too simple and naïve a disjunction between the two halves of this paragraph. That means, of course, that we must not too readily yield to the fashionable suggestion that in the Bible God appears as naïvely anthropomorphic, whereas in philosophy, especially in the Aristotelian tradition, he has lost all characteristics which might enable us to regard him as an object of worship and of personal confidence. Certainly, it is anachronistic, and reductive, to suggest that the Bible view of God can be summarized in some such description as 'God as personal'.

Nevertheless, it does remain true that the tension between biblical analogies and models on the one hand, and philosophical conceptions on the other hand, marks the traditional formulation of the doctrine of God. In the second paragraph of the chapter on God in the *Westminster Confession*, we may detect this tension.

'God hath all life, glory, goodness, blessedness, in and of himself; and is alone in and unto himself all-sufficient, not standing in need of any creatures which he hath made, not deriving any glory from them, but only manifesting his own glory, in, by, unto and upon them: he is the alone fountain of all being, of whom, through whom, and to whom, are all things; and hath most sovereign dominion over them, to do by them, for them, or upon them, whatsoever himself pleaseth. In his sight all things are open and manifest; his knowledge is infinite, infallible, and independent upon the creature, so as nothing is to him contingent or uncertain. He is most holy in all his counsels, in all his works and all his commands. To him is due from angels and men, and every other creature, whatsoever worship, service, or obedience, he is pleased to require of them.'

The sovereign freedom of God, which had already been simply detailed in paragraph one, is here expanded into what may almost be called a hymn to God's glory. But it is a hymn in terms of God's aseity, his being from himself and of himself. It is God's Being, God as the prime mover, himself unmoved and immovable, rather than the creator-redeemer, whose praise is here being sung. Or if the creator-redeemer does appear, in the descriptions of his glory, and in his sovereign dominion over all things, nevertheless, it is the all-sufficient God, the alone fountain of all being, who dominates the picture.

Only at the end, almost as an afterthought, in the brief final paragraph of this chapter, do we have a detached and laconic statement of orthodox Catholic teaching on the Trinity. And in succeeding chapters, which I do not need to detail, we find the awesome doctrine concerning God's eternal decree, with its teaching of double pre-destination, together with statements concerning creation and providence.

One major problem in the structure of the *Westminster Confession* comes out clearly in its treatment of the doctrine of God. I mean the ambiguity of the relation between its systematic formulations and Scripture itself. We may notice that in the matter of placing, the teaching about God comes after the teaching about Scripture. In the first chapter of the *Confession* we read of Scripture as 'given by inspiration of God, to be the rule of faith and life', and of God himself being the 'author thereof'. But, as I have already indicated, the content of the doctrine of God bears only a veneer of systematization. In fact it is a hotch-potch, in which the conceptions of the prime mover, of the creator-person, of the suprahistorical being and of the free and sovereign God manifesting his glory, jostle one another in a different kind of confusion from that of the Bible itself.

For of course Scripture contains the most kaleidoscopic and, for the calculating and rational mind, most bewildering collection of affirmations, images and models in its witness to God. This literary fact should make it clear that Scripture does not set out to elaborate a system of doctrine. In fact, it never seems to cross the minds of the biblical writers that the task of establishing a doctrine of God, or any kind of teaching about God, might be useful or fruitful or edifying for the matter of faith. Far less do we find any inclination on the part of the biblical writers to *prove* the existence of God—or to prove anything, for that matter.

It requires an intense effort of the imagination and of historical skill to transport oneself even to the threshold of the world of biblical apprehension and insight. It is true that the world-view of the biblical writers cannot simply be described as 'mythological'. It is, generally speaking, a world of 'broken' mythology which they inhabit, as Paul Tillich describes it.[1] That is to say, the tension of distance and nearness, of an external spec-

[1] 'Mythologie' in *Religion in Geschichte und Gegenwart*, 2nd ed.

tatorial attitude in tension with an exclusive experience of being plunged into the very heart of life in a much more undifferentiated way, is very evident in the Old Testament world in particular. Yet even when we recognize this peculiar tension, in which it was possible, and indeed necessary, to speak of God as both near and far off, we are still at an immense remove from the later theologizing of the Christian Church.

Thus the realm of discourse which was later to be separated off as that of 'natural theology' in distinction from 'revealed theology'—and then later still permitted to wander off as an independent discipline, related only to man's rational systematization of his cosmic yearnings —this realm of natural theology never played any significant part in the story of Israel's self-understanding. For their understanding of themselves and their destiny was throughout a matter of presenting the consequences of their faith in a God who, however he might be experienced—as judgment, or forbearance, or loving-kindness —was never doubted to be a real and active power in the midst of Israel's history. How then, in such circumstances, could what the Christian Church knows as theology arise in the life and religious experience of Israel?

Scripture, to put it briefly, does not deal in dogmas. This is not to say that it is confined to a religious sphere of life. The religious experience of Israel was of such a kind that neither theology nor religion is an adequate conceptual tool for understanding it. The nearest we can get to understanding the way in which Israel's life proceeded is to think of it in terms of history: it was man's total historical existence before God which was both the setting and the substance for the biblical writers. In this existence God was not a part of the world, who could be inferred within it by a process of the discursive reason. Nor was he an object to be considered, again by means of an analysis of the phenomena. But he was the active Lord of their history, in their history and constituting that history.

In fact, the distinction between Scripture and the subsequent Christian theological tradition is so sharp that it might seem perverse to speak of both elements as 'tradition'. Nevertheless, the distinction is not ultimate. Both Scripture and later theological formulations may be described alike as part of the tradition, because over against them there stands the reality of faith. Not even Scripture has a paradigmatic function for faith. Certainly, the biblical tradition is permanently at odds with the later fatal tendency to standardize the content of faith as a system of reflective, discursive and objective theologizing. But in itself the biblical tradition is something more than a polemical counterpart to a theological tradition which in fact only arose on the basis of the biblical tradition. But the biblical tradition is nothing in itself. It would be a double fatality if we regarded ourselves as forced into a position where we merely had to reiterate the attitudes and thought-forms of the Bible. Rather, the Christian tradition, firmly based upon the same historical existence as that of the biblical writers, has to learn ever again to look with the biblical writers in the same direction as they do. To attempt any simple imitation, or repristination, of their modes and styles is to succumb to a pathetic form of the literalist heresy. There is no way of returning to the world of the Bible. The only possible way forward is to learn from the biblical writers and then to go our own way.

In Richard Niebuhr's words: 'A history that was recorded forwards, as it were, must be read backwards through our history if it is to be understood as revelation.'[1]

To return to our consideration of the doctrine of God as expounded in the *Westminster Confession of Faith*: what the *Confession* does with God is to reduce him to the object of systematic thought. Or rather, it attempts to do this. Certainly, it succeeds in making clear that God is not to be found in the world—but this also means that God is not to be found in the *Westminster Confession* either.

It might well be asked at this point whether a too forceful critique of all theological enquiry might not render the task of theology simply impossible. For if no objectifying and systematizing work is permissible, on the grounds that this makes God into a part of the world, either as an object within it or as the slave of a system elaborated by the systematic theologian, who thus can be regarded as having God more or less at his mercy—if no effort of this kind is permissible, but is regarded as illegitimate in respect of the subject-matter, namely, the free and absolute God—then it might well be asked whether there was any legitimate way of discoursing about God left. Karl Barth has seen the problem with

[1] *The Meaning of Revelation*, Macmillan, New York, 1946, p. 50.

excruciating clarity. This is the reason for his passionate rejection of all natural theology. But when this rejection involves, as I believe it does, a thoroughgoing scepticism concerning the whole world in which not only natural theology, but also man in his historicity, is to be found, then it is imperative to look for some other way in which, with all necessary regard for the difference between God and man, nevertheless the conjunction of God and man is not merely recognized as a brilliant intellectual re-mapping of experience, but is actually embodied at the heart of theological discourse. This other way is what will concern us in the outcome of these lectures.

What we face here once again is what I have already described as the tragedy inherent in all temporal efforts to fix the eternal. The more powerful the attempt at systematic coherence, the more self-contained the system, the greater the final failure.

The question which today hangs over the whole classical procedure of the Church's formulations of its history and experience is whether it is not always bound to end as a contradiction of its original purpose.

When the place of confessions, in particular, comes to be discussed in ecumenical contexts, it seems to me that there can be as little doubt about the permanent historical value of the various confessions as about their present-day ineffectuality for the purposes for which they were framed. Or rather, the real purposes for which they were framed involved the recognition that they were entirely non-normative. For our own time, so weak is the systematic urge, and so tender the plant of faith, that it seems necessary to aim rather at too little than at too much in the way of confession. 'Jesus is Lord' is enough to divide the spirits.

The practical failure of the traditional method of theologizing, as exemplified in the contradictions inherent in any attempt to present a doctrine of God, reflects the crisis in belief. The crisis in belief is so closely connected with the methodological crisis that each may be called a function of the other. Now that this double crisis is actually upon us, it is possible to see how it has arrived with a kind of fatality in the long course of Western theology. The main outline of the position was already adumbrated by Hegel.

The negative side of what Hegel wrote about the death of God has been taken up by the contemporary so-called 'death-of-God theologians'. For Hegel showed that it was no longer possible to cling to the idea of God as the sustainer of values, or as the originator of movement.

Hegel's positive solution, or construction, found in man's history a dialectical movement which ended in the absolute spirit, conceived as identical with man's spirit. The 'absolute truth', 'totality of meaning' and 'ground' are thus experienced in Hegel's system as a historical reality.[1]

From two points of view Hegel's thought exposes the impossibility of the traditional dogmatic theology. Classic natural theology ends, fittingly enough, in Hegel's

[1] cf. W. D. Marsch, *Die Gegenwart Christi*, Kaiser Verlag, Munich, 1965, p. 237.

synthesis: that is, in absolute thought, without move-ment. This is the side of Hegel which Kierkegaard per-ceived so clearly, and rejected with such merciless wit. But secondly, when Hegel speaks of 'God's showing himself in the historical situation', he is aware of 'the infinite pain of a loss which . . . makes us ask about resurrection'. Hegel's own system, so far as it seeks to arrest the unpredictable dynamism of God's historical self-disclosures, is incapable of dealing satisfactorily with the very question which history itself, as he says, raises: the question of resurrection. But far less is the traditional dogmatic and normative theology capable of dealing with this question. For God, regarded as an object to be known, as an extension of the immanent natural world, is not the living Lord of Christian faith.

The impasse is unmistakable. Is it also insurmountable? Is there no way of expressing a faith in God which is simultaneously rational and able to suffer the surprises of contingent existence?

Strictly speaking, this crisis about God is a crisis of method, a crisis in our hermeneutical procedures which is at the same time (as I have said) a crisis of belief. The way through this crisis, as I see it, is by a restoration of the self-understanding of faith. In this restoration both belief itself, and the way in which we set about under-standing and expressing it, are dealt with together, as the unity which they in fact are.

That is to say, as Kierkegaard said of Hegel that in a fit of absent-mindedness he left out movement from his system, we may say that to leave faith out, to forget faith, is bound to leave us with an attenuated conception of reason as our only guide.

It would be absurd to resuscitate at this point the hoary discussion about the relations of faith and reason. It should be clear that, whatever the actual success of such an undertaking as the present enquiry, I certainly desiderate the restoration of the power of the autonomous reason to a proper functioning in the whole matter of theological discussion. Theology, after all, is meant to be rational discourse about God.

This does not mean, however, that we must at once subscribe to some alleged norm for understanding how this discourse is to be conducted. The demands equally of some modern philosophers and theologians can only be faced with the same kind of sharp, but I hope not uncharitable, remark as that which Barth used for the death-of-God theologians: 'Unkultur'.

It is much truer to the present state of affairs to see that there is a great deal of confusion about the place of natural theology. The question of its possibility at all has, as every theological student knows, and as every philosophy professor professes to know, been answered with a decided negative by Karl Barth, and with a qualified negative by Emil Brunner, by Rudolf Bultmann and by others of the dominant theological schools.

The question of natural theology must be faced in terms of a fresh assessment of the claim of faith. So long as natural theology is assumed to be an activity of the human reason working entirely independent of, and without any reference to, the gift and the historical human reality of faith as an actual experience, there is bound to be a clash: a conflict of assumptions which simply cannot be resolved. And without a broadening and deepening of our definition of the scope and activity of reason, I do not see how we are going to escape from the melancholy impasse in which philosophy and theology, ostensibly concerned with the same object, namely, man in his whole world, scarcely even notice one another's existence.

> The claims of certain philosophical analysts show how severe the impasse is. Thus Carl Michalson rightly says that 'the verification which positivism required has nothing in common with theological reasoning. Specific facts, which are surely no sufficient cause of religious belief, are no necessary cause either. To say so underestimates the radical effect which personal belief with its intentionality has upon the logic of reality with which faith is involved.'[1] What Michalson is basically referring to is the scope of faith, and thus the special logic it requires. Faith is primarily, as he rightly says, 'an historical reality', whereas analytic philosophy is not really interested in history. Far less is it interested in tragedy. Thus he quotes A. J. Ayer as recently deploring the fact that certain philosophers 'see tragedy in what could not conceivably be otherwise'. Michalson interprets this to mean that some philosophers cannot 'live with equanimity in the presence of the inability to know anything for certain'. However, tragic awareness, or the lack of it where it might seem appropriate, is less a matter of knowing or not knowing, and more a matter of one's total response to life's circumstances. Michalson's whole essay ('Linguistic Analysis and the Context of Faith') deserves study.

[1] Carl Michalson, *Worldly Theology*, pp. 46 f.

66

Perhaps it is chiefly the other, more old-fashioned style of philosophy—that which is on the whole represented by the Gifford-Lecturer tradition—from which there may be most hope of a real dialogue with theology. In one sense this may be rather a surprising hope, since it is the traditional metaphysical school which has long worked with a narrow understanding of reason and has settled its accounts with faith by tending to equate faith with mysticism or mystical experience of the respectable kind which is the stock-in-trade (or is at least regarded as such) of writers like Rudolf Otto, with his idea of the 'numinous'. This leaves them free to pursue their old course, with the neat delimitation of spheres, in which, however, the tacit assumption is that reason, understood as an autonomous power, itself has the sole right to establish what is reasonable. On this basis, certainly, and with its implied epistemology, the reasonable procedure of this kind of philosophy ends with a God who is just an object among other objects in the world. In other words, with a refined agnosticism. I am not suggesting that a better procedure would be that of the philosophical theologians, for they, starting from the same premises as their companions, the theologically minded philosophers, usually end with unacceptable claims for the normative status of a doctrine of God which has evacuated the mystery and has made an illegitimate attempt to secure the unsecurable.

What seems in fact to be required is an extension of the view of what is the proper scope and possibility of human reason. The kind of natural theology which has hitherto been regarded as permissible and valid, within the traditional division of spheres between the place of reason and the place of faith, has been in effect the exercise of reason within an unreasonably limited field.

So far as this operation of reason includes the observing, thinking agent himself, it is bound to end in self-adulation or in resignation. For this inclusion of himself means no more than the inclusion of the 'objective' experiences accessible to the introspective powers of his own reason. Under the guise of being rational and objective, the unfortunate philosopher is caught in the toils of his own narrowly posited reason.

To speak of self-adulation, or 'boasting', as St Paul called it, or of resignation, does not in the least imply a moral judgment. I am not pronouncing judgment from an unassailable *cathedra*, but merely making a phenomenological observation on the consequences of this particular understanding of the scope of reason.

Karl Barth was not so polite. As I have already had occasion to remark, he spoke of natural theology as 'the anti-Christ'. He is usually regarded by philosophers as indulging his undoubted polemical powers at the expense of a rational equipoise. However, in view of the vacillation of the Church against the claims of Nazi mythology, and in view of the temporizing of his colleagues—including his philosophy colleagues—in the German universities, it might be admitted, even by philosophers, that a certain lack of equipoise was the only way to draw attention to the pressing dangers in the political and social situation.

Certainly, in the context of our own discussion we may now say that a view of reason which omits the self-understanding of faith from its purview is committing a serious historical fallacy. For Christ is the source of faith. Can Christ be extruded from the sphere of reasonable consideration? If he were a centaur, or even directly and plainly a god on earth, he could well be left out of account. But the history of understanding, the herme-neutical tradition, regarding Christ, cannot be so easily disposed of. For it is not enough to relegate the story of Christ to the area of thought traditionally known as 'revealed theology'. Christ is a historical phenomenon who has, to say the least, the most remarkable reper-cussions upon, and interactions with, so-called natural theology.

In the history of man's self-understanding the relation-ships between the two activities—that is, natural and revealed theology—are so close that the modern assump-tion of a complete diremption between the two parts can only be described as a historical fallacy. The allocation of spheres of interest, so to speak, was rapidly interpreted as meaning that the one sphere could operate without the other: and especially that the sphere of natural theology, and then the whole power of the autonomous reason, was sufficient to cope with the whole situation of man. This is the particular tragedy of the development of rationalism since the Enlightenment, that it has been content to define itself on such a narrow basis that vast areas of experience and of historical self-understanding have been excluded, thrown to the wolves of fortune.

But man's history is not at the mercy of the goddess Fortuna. The only hope for man is that Fortuna should be destroyed, and trust in destiny substituted.

In fairness both to the philosopher and the theologian it must be added that it is easy to see how the divorce between them has come about. The main cause has been the growing autonomy of the activities of Western society in a state of what Dilthey has aptly described as 'free manifoldness'. And among these activities reason has also won its independence. Unfortunately, however, this independence has come to be regarded as carrying with it a conception of reason which is content to exclude certain of the historical phenomena. In other words, the reason of the philosopher sets certain specific limits to the phenomena regarded as reasonable. The devotees of revealed religion have responded by withdrawing these same phenomena from circulation. The one side has so played into the hands of the other that the delimitation of spheres has hardened into almost impenetrable barriers.

If I have so far given the impression that I am speaking from one side—the side of 'revelation theology'—against the other side—the side of 'natural theology'—let me correct this impression by saying that I regard the blame for the situation (if we may speak thus crudely) as being perhaps more attributable to the theologians who for too many generations have been apt to claim for the tenets of their faith a position either 'beyond' or 'outside' or (more commonly) 'against' reason. It has as a consequence been only too easy for the 'rational' philosophers to dismiss the claims of Christian faith as 'irrational'.

The whole problem needs a fresh approach. Is there not another way of understanding the nature of revealed theology, and the status of natural theology? The substance of what I have to say in later lectures about man's historicity will, I hope, provide the material for a revised understanding of revealed theology. Meantime, I should suggest that natural theology, in its essential intention, is not an alternative to revealed or 'supernatural' theology. The two are not mutually exclusive competitors for the job of dealing with man's historical reality. Rather, in Karl Rahner's words, natural theology is to be understood as 'an inner element in revelation theology itself'.[1] Or, in the words of another Roman Catholic theologian, E. Schillebeeckx, 'the theological concept "nature", as distinguished from "supernature", does not refer to the Aristotelian category, but is an intrinsic implication of revelation itself'.[2] If we say that in theology 'nature' 'need not refer', rather than 'does not refer', to the Aristotelian category, then the way begins to open out.

But this is not the way merely to a positivist fideism, in place of the previous allocation of spheres of interest, or in place of the once fruitful tension between faith and reason. That is to say, we cannot simply choose faith instead of reason, revelation and supernature instead of the discoveries of the unaided human effort, and develop a theology of revelation which is simply a positivist

[1] *The Word in History*, ed. T. Patrick Burke, Collins, London, 1968, p. 9.
[2] Ibid., p. 42.

repetition of truths of faith. With such a method we should merely find ourselves back in the familiar field which we had already left. Only now, instead of being faced with a normative theology which sought to combine philosophical understanding with Christian traditional material (as in the *Westminster Confession of Faith*), we should be faced with a normative theology which was based entirely upon a repetition of biblical affirmations.

It is probably a melancholy necessity of our time to repeat what I have already said more than once—that the normative historical power is not and cannot be any traditional documents, not even the Bible, but is solely the person of Christ. Therefore, it is a methodological error of the first order to suppose that Christianity is based upon a book, and that a true theology is one which discovers what the Bible says and then re-asserts this in a 'modern' fashion—but all the same, basically just repeats what the Bible says. We are not going to duck out from under the claims of our own historicity and rationality as easily as that.

The way through the entire impasse is by means of the recognition that faith is not an isolated phenomenon. Faith is never alone. But it is a gift which is given in our situation, as an event.

The givenness of faith is basic. A relationship is not, so to speak, excogitated; but it is given. The gift involves us in the relationship with the giver.

Faith, therefore, makes sense only when it is seen as involving the believer's understanding of himself as not alone, but as bound up in relationships. Thus there is no line of demarcation between the reality of faith and the understanding of faith. Faith is real, is truly itself, in so far as it is grasped as involving the givenness and the relationship.

This is the point at which we are able to speak of natural theology once again. It is the nature of man, as bound up with and expressed in the gift of faith, which now requires to be examined in all its possibilities. These possibilities range far beyond the question of theoretical possibilities and include the way in which a man becomes what he can become.

In this context the doctrine of God becomes comprehensible once more, but now in terms of a doctrine of man. Of course, in an analogous way the doctrine of man can only be explicated in terms of the doctrine of God. For faith is now understood, it understands itself, as the junction between God and man: faith, that is to say, which is recognized as both illuminating man's pre-reflexive self-understanding and as guiding man's reflection upon his new existence in faith.

Faith, in brief, becomes material for man's reason to work upon and can be regarded as the substance by which man's essential rationality is displayed.

The impression must not be gained, from this description of faith, that God is merely the echo of man's self-understanding. It is a common and cheap criticism of an existentialist analysis of faith that it is merely a description of man's own inwardness, of his subjective experience, and the like. The classic document of self-confident mis-

73

understanding in our time, so far as theology is concerned, is Karl Barth's essay entitled, with a modesty which belies its contents, 'Rudolf Bultmann: Ein Versuch ihn zu verstehen' ('Rudolf Bultmann, an attempt to understand him'). A more accurate title would be 'An illustration of how thoroughly it is possible to misunderstand another writer'.

All that has so far been suggested for faith is that it has a claim to be regarded as a historical reality, open to the exercise of our reason. From the standpoint of theology, this means that a theological anthropology, rather than a dogmatic theology, deserves to be examined. Along the lines of such an enquiry we may hope for a fresh understanding of the meaning to be attached to the word 'God'.

In any case, along the lines of the traditional theology we have reached a dead end. Christianity is no longer effectively regarded as 'a religion looking for a metaphysic', as Whitehead once called it. But it is a faith looking for a structure of understanding.

If this empirical and phenomenological approach is sound, it means that God can be determined from within the historical situation of man. Can God be determined *only* from within this situation? Certainly, in our time, and standing as we do at the end of over a thousand years of enquiry into God as an object, the possibility of genuine talk of faith, or of revelation, or of God, seems to depend upon what can be found within our empirical experience. What other source have we but our experience?

THE CRISIS ABOUT GOD

God, then, if he is expressible at all, belongs to the
definition of man. But this does not mean, once again,
man defined as external, that is to say, as an object, to
himself; but man in his relatedness.

'. . . the world of human experience is the only access to the
saving reality of revelation and faith. For that matter, how
could we listen to a revelation from God—how can it be a
revelation to man, if it falls outside our experience? It is
impossible for man to know or be aware of realities which
he does not experience in some way or another.'[1]

One last thing must be said, and indeed it runs through
all that I have said about the present crisis: it is the
mystery of God. One of the basic requirements of all
attempts to talk about God must be a much more
consistent application of the procedures of the *via negativa*.
By this I mean more than the application of the traditional
negative theological method in order to say what God is
not—a procedure which subtly implies that we are after
all making some kind of affirmation. Rather, a more
thoroughgoing agnosticism is implied here: we must say
that we cannot say what God is. In the conception of God
as being not the world and not man an unbounded
mystery is indicated. Even more, an unbounded mystery
can be experienced, and is experienced.

This, which is still a human experience, yet points
beyond all knowledge, is, paradoxically, the real justifi-

[1] E. Schillebeeckx, 'Faith and Self-Understanding', in *The Word in
History*, ed. T. Patrick Burke, p. 45. I am happy to acknowledge not
merely this quotation, but a great deal of stimulus for the whole
argument of this chapter, to Fr Schillebeeckx's essay.

cation for all fresh attempts at giving its due place to some kind of natural theology. For here, in the sheer givenness of human experience, there is a question—we may call it with Fr Schillebeeckx 'a pre-reflexive or un-thematic self-understanding'[1]—which has of course fuller answers, combined with the knowledge gained by faith, but which also has, as the strong undertow of all human existence, the answer which comes out of the abyss of the mystery of God.

Does this mean that fundamentally the question which is addressed to the mystery of man's givenness—a question addressed by man to man—can never be answered by man at all? Does it mean that only God can both contain and express the absoluteness of the answer? Rather, I should say that an absolute disjunction between God and man is not the last stage in the relation between God and man. What is possible and open to man is that he should be able to face the mystery. So in the end it is not *what* he can say about God in his in-effability, but *how* he faces him, that is able to express simultaneously both man and God.

But this cannot mean anything else but an ultimate self-abandonment by man in face of the mystery whom we call God.

'The essence of Christianity is in the question about *how* one becomes a Christian. Christian faith is not a teaching about God but a mode of existence.'[2]

To sum up these reflections on the crisis about God, we

[1] Ibid., p. 44.
[2] Carl Michalson, *Worldly Theology*, p. 117.

find that the only possible way out of the present state of affairs is through a deeper analysis of the reality of our human experience of faith. And this deeper analysis must take full account both of the failure of the objectifying and systematizing theology of traditional method and of the powers inherent in the self-understanding of faith and in the decision for Christian obedience. The truth lies in that kind of subjectivity which is expressed in the Johannine words, 'I am the way, the truth, and the life'.

CHAPTER THREE

God as Being

In my examination of what I called the crisis about God I described it as a crisis of method, a crisis in hermeneutical procedure. The traditional formulation of the doctrine of God, together with the kind of claim for acceptance, holding it to be true, which has generally been attached to it, has in effect defined God out of existence. The way faith has been understood has more and more tended to leave out the trusting confrontation which is the very heart of faith. Thus God has been objectified, and acceptance of the doctrine concerning him has been pressed as being necessary in such a way that today, when conditions have changed so rapidly in so many different ways, both the definition and the demand for its acceptance have alike become highly dubious.

The kind of objectivity that is left in modern man's view of the world is so problematic that it is no help, but a positive hindrance, to the understanding of God that he should be traditionally presented as an accessible object in the world.

Actual belief in God, again, has been traditionally so tied up with an objective doctrine of God that the crisis concerning the doctrine necessarily involves a crisis concerning the belief.

In what way this twofold crisis may be understood actually to bring about as it were a dissolution of the reality of God, is a further question which can only be properly faced when we tackle the problem of just how, in what positive terms and with what positive implications, we succeed in framing a modern doctrine and offer a reasonable way of understanding what belief in God is, that is, what it entails.

If no such positive terms and positive implications can be found; if, that is to say, there is no other reliable way of approaching God, or of recognizing that he is approaching us, than the traditional way, then it would certainly, in my view, be time to write *finis* across the story of God with man. God could then be relegated to the region of primitive mythology, and be cultivated in private by a dwindling company of romantics and introverts.

Now I think it is on the whole true to say that, whatever the state of affairs in the churches, or in the world in general, there is among modern theologians a fairly general consensus that God cannot be described as *a* being. That he can be so described has been the traditional assumption of natural theology. On the whole, at least, I think it is fair to say that traditional theology has regarded God as one entity among others, certainly the supreme entity, but one who can be demonstrated to exist and to possess certain comprehensible attributes. But the way of understanding God has certainly not been so simple a matter, in the history of theology, as sometimes appears in the generalizations to which we are all prone. Thus the whole weight of so-called truths of revelation is bound to come down on the side of a view of God as one who, even if he cannot simply be described as a being, nevertheless is not adequately described as Being, and not even as 'Holy Being'. He is, within the Christian story, confessed as the God and Father of our Lord Jesus Christ. In what sense is this confession tied up with the idea of a personal being? Whether this description has to give way, in the end, to some other which can claim greater comprehensiveness and reality, is precisely the question at issue. It cannot be answered on any other basis but that which is provided by the whole ensemble of our experience.

While, therefore, we may agree with the fairly general discrediting of the view of God as a being, in so far as that description reduces God to being within the world, as an object, we must reserve our discussion of what we mean by the reality of God for when we come to examine the nature of his historicity in Christ.

This does not mean, of course, that we wish to resolve our problem by simply calling revelation to our aid. This does not indeed mean very much until it has been explained just what we mean by revelation. And if by revelation is meant a package deal of saving communications, or even of saving actions, running against the stream of human possibilities, and especially running contrary to man's rational apprehensions, then this kind of recourse is, it seems to me, unable to carry conviction in modern experience. This kind of revelation is as inaccessible to modern unitary styles of existence and understanding as is the kind of reason which produces God at the end of a syllogism.

If it be retorted, then so much the worse for modern human existence and styles of apprehension, in such a case there can be no further fruitful discussion between representatives of two such opposing positions. For positivism in theology, of a kind which wishes to write off human history and culture as either meaningless or merely sinful, and is in either case not inclined to hear any word of God except what is given in the form of authoritative communications, has not even begun to grasp the historical reality which it is, in the Christian understanding, the very destiny of God, in love, to undergo. Revelational positivism leaves out the ultimate —not fictional, not temporary, not pretended, but unreserved and ultimate—reality of God's suffering love in Christ. It is this reality, in all its helpless humanity, which —for all modern men's insensitivity to the Christian tradition in its subtler nuances—is still able to rise up and confront men in the midst of all kinds of authentic human situations.

One other serious reply to the general question about how it is possible to speak of God today is that which derives from the classic affirmation of God as Being. This is not an easy affirmation to disentangle from the more complex tradition. It is certainly to be found in traditional Thomist exposition. (This, however, is disputed by

Martin Heidegger, in so far as he regards mediaeval theology as representing the newer metaphysical tradition. We may understand Heidegger to be conscious of a reality in Being, which is something more than the reality of beings. When he talks of being '*gestreift*', grazed, by Being, we may take him at his word, however hard it may be to elucidate. At least Heidegger is here claiming to be pointing to a real personal experience. And further-more, we must surely agree that Thomas Aquinas has somehow in mind the reality of beings, primarily; but does this exclude Being?)

The tradition of philosophizing about Being, *pace* Heidegger, is nevertheless to be found through the whole story of Western philosophy and theology. In traditional theological discourse the theme of God as Being is so firmly entrenched that a full examination of it would involve us in a survey of the whole history of theology.

It is my intention to abstract from the complex story one particular matter, namely, the biblical understanding of God as Being. The conclusion of my examination will be that in one important sense the biblical view does not permit an unqualified affirmation of God as one who is for himself and of himself. This conclusion opens the way to a re-statement of what then in biblical faith, and in modern terms, can be meaningfully said about God's being.

Nevertheless, I do not intend to press my conclusion in such a way as to exclude some kind of concordat with philosophical theology. For in the last analysis it would be a gesture of despair to rest content with the disjunction between the God of the philosophers and the God of Abraham, Isaac and Jacob.

Thus Emil Brunner exposes the ultimate scepticism of his particular kind of revelation theology when he contends that theology is not interested in the god of the philosophers.[1]

But it cannot be denied that the difficulties of combining the two ways of speaking—and thus of thinking, and of living—are extreme.

The special difficulty may be illustrated in the neo-Thomism of such a severe and admirable scholar as Professor Eric Mascall. He writes as follows:

'Aquinas sees God's fundamental attribute as self-subsistent being (*Summa contra Gentiles* I, x, 1: "The selfsame thing which God is, is his existence") . . . His starting-point is "the metaphysic of Exodus", the revelation of the name of God as "I am that I am" . . . And the conception of God as *ipsum esse subsistens*, subsistent being itself, is fundamental to his whole discussion of the divine nature.'

Professor Mascall adds in a footnote that 'It should be noted that St Thomas does not *state* that self-existent being is the formal constituent of deity. It is, however, widely held that this was his view.'[2]

[1] *Revelation and Reason*, SCM Press, London, 1947:
   'The God of the philosophers is a God who has been "thought"; He is not the Lord God. The God of philosophy is an abstraction; He is not "the Living God". The Living God is not known through thought . . . ; He is known through revelation alone. The Lord God is the God of biblical revelation.' (p. 44.)
   'There is no connection between natural theology and the biblical knowledge of God; this we say without reserve.' (p. 61.)
[2] Eric Mascall, *He Who Is*, Longmans, London, 1943, p. 13

In a recent essay of Professor Karl Rahner, however, there is an important difference of emphasis. Thus he writes:

'God's act of love to us, precisely because it is God's act and not ours (though, of course, it frees us not only to have things done to us but also to do things) must be thought of as coming before our act of love and faith and making this act possible, and thus, inevitably, it must be thought of in categories of being—state, accident, habit, infusion, etc.'[1]

It is clear that Professor Rahner wishes still to regard the *ipsum esse*—being itself—as basic, and this being means for him that the familiar mediaeval categories of being are required in order to make sense of God's act. But at the same time the conception of God as acting has taken a central place: God as *actus purus* is seen as the God who is also self-subsistent being. The supreme being is thus understood as the cause of all finite beings. The union of the two ideas—*ipsum esse* and *actus purus*—is the basic formulation of mediaeval theology, which seeks to combine in a rational unity the absoluteness of self-subsistent being with historical acts done through finite creaturely existence. It remains a question whether, even on its own terms, mediaeval theology has succeeded in establishing a unity of being and act. The God who is *actus purus* is a God who actualizes himself, and who is actual, in his acts. Has his being, then, apart from his acts, any meaning? If we object that such a being has no

[1] Karl Rahner, *Nature and Grace*, Sheed and Ward, 1963, paperbacked., p. 25.

content, it may still be said that no content is in fact claimed for it: self-existent being is the *formal* constituent. This would presumably leave room for God's acts to be the content of his being.

But to understand God's being primarily in terms of his acts is not the traditional way of regarding the problem. What God is, rather than what he does, has been the object of attention. The *ipsum esse* has been regarded as basic, and the *actus purus* retreats behind the affirmation of the absoluteness of God's being of himself. But this is the philosopher's God—or at least the God of one kind of philosopher: uncaused, self-subsistent, needing nothing apart from himself to remain unchangeably himself.

We may see this traditional concern in play in the work of a typical post-Hegelian idealist theologian, Isaak Dorner. Thus he writes:

'If God refuses to allow us any knowledge of His Being in itself, but only of His Being in its relation to the world, then He reveals to the world, because not Himself, necessarily some other than Himself.'[1]

Here again the emphasis has shifted. For Dorner the chief question is the relation of revelation—regarded as 'that which has been revealed'—to God in himself. Dorner requires some kind of initial certainty that what is revealed is God's being in itself. It would seem that he is asking for more than even the mediaeval schoolmen wished to have: for now the *ipsum esse* appears, in

[1] Isaak Dorner, *System der Christlichen Glaubenslehre*, Vol. I, 1886, p. 191.

Dorner's view, to be the content as well as the form of the deity. Being is everything; and act has become merely a coda to this self-sufficient all of the divine being.

To the ambiguities in this position we shall address ourselves later, when we come to ask what the historical revelation in Christ implies for our understanding of God and for our way of speaking of him. In view of the widely held opinion, however, that Thomas Aquinas represents a peculiar metaphysic of being, scripturally linked with the so-called 'metaphysic of Exodus', it is pertinent to note the increasing tendency among Thomist scholars to question this understanding of Thomas. Thus J. B. Metz, in an important essay, entitled 'The Church and the World', expresses full agreement with modern Old Testament exegetes in respect of the meaning of Exodus 3: 14, and adds: 'According to this version God revealed himself to Moses more as the power of the future than as a being dwelling beyond all history and experience . . . His transcendence reveals itself as our "absolute future".'[1]

It may therefore be not too forced an exegesis of Thomas which sees in him less the proponent of 'static' being, of the unmoved mover, the unhistorical source, and the like, and more the Christian theologian who was 'brushed by Being', as Heidegger puts it,[2] and forced by this experience to ask about how finite beings

[1] *The Word in History*, p. 76.
[2] *Introduction to Metaphysics*, translated by Ralph Manheim, OUP, London, 1959, p. 1. His exact words are 'grazed at least once . . . by the hidden power of this question' (*scil.* of Being).

move at all, rather than to ask about Being as sufficient to itself.[1]

The position of Karl Barth, so far as it may be extracted from his voluminous writings and presented in a consistent form, is of particular interest to us at this point. The elegant essay by Eberhard Jüngel, 'Gottes Sein ist im Werden' ('God's being is in becoming') is, I think, a reliable exposition of Barth's general view. In what follows I am indebted to Professor Jüngel for the main outlines, but not for the conclusion.

For Barth the primary reality of God is in God's relationship to himself, that is, in his intra-trinitarian being. Only after the establishment of this order of being does Barth speak of God in relation to the world:

'He [God] becomes living for us . . . only as He enters into relation with us, as there stands over against Him a world and especially man in his manifold movement, in relation to which He Himself acquires movement. But He cannot be taken with true and final seriousness in this movement, and therefore in His glory, His glory cannot be accepted strictly . . . That God is mighty, holy, just, merciful, omnipresent, is affirmed more in relation to an analogical world in which He exists for us, than in relation to His being in itself as it is in reality.'[2]

Now when Barth speaks, as he does here, of God's relation to the world and man as not to be taken 'with

[1] For these summary remarks about the understanding of St Thomas Aquinas, I am also indebted to Fr Columba Ryan for an unpublished paper.
[2] Karl Barth, *Church Dogmatics*, II. 1, T. and T. Clark, Edinburgh, 1957, p. 324.

true and final seriousness', it is difficult to avoid the conclusion that there is a strong note of scepticism in his view
of man's relation to God. It is true that later in the same
paragraph Barth does assert the identity of God in
himself and God as he gives himself in his revelation.
The assurance of this identity, however, is simply made
to depend upon the assurances of Scripture. Thus he
writes:

'It is dangerous and ultimately fatal to faith in God if God
is not the Lord of glory, if it is not guaranteed to us that in
spite of the analogical nature of the language in which it all
has to be expressed God is actually and unreservedly as we
encounter Him in His revelation: the Almighty, the Holy,
the Just, the Merciful, the Omnipresent, the Eternal, not less
but infinitely more so than it is in our power to grasp, and
not for us only, but in actuality therefore in Himself. Holy
Scripture speaks to us of God in such a way as to give us this
assurance. It does not point beyond the whole glory of God
to this punctual or linear being, as though the latter is the
real and true God, while His glory is only a mode of revelation, a phenomenon. But attesting to us the glory of God, it
certifies to us that this Lord of glory is as such the real and
true God.'[1]

'When we ask questions about God's being, we cannot in fact
leave the sphere of His action and working as it is revealed to
us in His Word. . . . In the light of what He is in His works
it is no longer an open question what He is in Himself. In
Himself He cannot, perhaps, be someone or something quite
other, or perhaps nothing at all. But in His works He is
Himself revealed as the One He is.'[2]

[1] Ibid., p. 325.
[2] Ibid., p. 260; cf. H. Gollwitzer, *The Existence of God*, SCM Press, London, 1965, p. 27.

This assurance, however, as Professor Jüngel's essay makes clear, does not carry Barth's thought into the possibilities of a being of God which is based upon the primacy of historical revelation. Rather, God's being is understood as basically 'ein selbstbezogenes Sein', a self-related Being, and this is the 'primary objectivity of God',[1] namely, within the life of the Trinity. 'Because [God] is first and foremost knowable to Himself as the triune God, He is knowable to us as well.'[2] God's objectivity, therefore, in his revelation is 'secondary objectivity'. Thus in his relation with men in the revelation through Christ, God is 'in action', accessible, *'auf dem Plan'* only in his work, which points as a sign to him.

We can therefore, according to Professor Jüngel's paraphrase of Barth, understand God's being essentially as being which is relational in a twofold sense. 'That is, God can enter into relation with another (*ad extra*) (and precisely in this relation can his being exist ontically, without ontological dependence on this other), because God's being (*ad intra*) is a self-related being.'[3]

Professor Jüngel makes a strenuous effort to rescue Barth's view on the one hand from sheer scepticism, and on the other hand from sheer relationalism. To find a way of asserting simultaneously the absolute difference of God from everything else, and his relation to everything else, without diminution of the difference, is without any doubt the key problem for theological thought.

[1] E. Jüngel, *Gottes Sein ist im Werden*, Tübingen, 1965, p. 72; cf. Barth *Church Dogmatics*, II. 1, pp. 39 f.
[2] *Church Dogmatics*, II. 1, pp. 67 f.
[3] E. Jüngel, op. cit., p. 111.

While it is temerarious of me, on the slight evidence I have drawn from Barth and from Professor Jüngel's paraphrase of Barth, to venture a different interpretation, I cannot avoid the impression, which Professor Jüngel's interpretation does not extinguish but indeed unwittingly strengthens, that Barth is relying basically upon a specific philosophy of being, namely, that of an intra-trinitarian reality, self-related, primary and aloof. The world and man and revelation are left in a secondary and ambiguous state. From the ultimate scepticism which this disjunction tends to force upon the apprehension, Barth escapes only by means of faith in the biblical tradition as something given to us definitively. Barth moves into the realm of assurance about man and the world and revelation by means of what Bonhoeffer called his 'positivism of revelation'.[1] Barth's *analogia fidei*, the analogy of faith, by means of which he endeavours to maintain the connection between the historical revelation and the intra-trinitarian reality which is in his view the primary, 'objective' and controlling reality, can now be seen as an ultimately unsupported fideism. Certainly, Barth *wishes* to move wholly within the realm of faith and grace, and this is what gives extraordinary vigour to his position. It also provides it with a certain pathos. For by means of this analogy he wishes to move back into the anthropomorphic, intensely relational world of biblical faith. But

[1] See Dietrich Bonhoeffer, *Letters and Papers from Prison*, revised edition, SCM Press, London, 1967, p. 153; also the essay by Regin Prenter on 'Bonhoeffer and Barth's Positivism of Revelation' in *World Come of Age*, ed. R. Gregor Smith, Collins, 1967, pp. 93 ff.

the reality of God remains apart from the self-under-standing of faith.

In Barth we have the last, and possibly the greatest, certainly an awe-inspiring, effort on the part of traditional metaphysical theology to overcome the difficulty of relating 'God in his being for himself' with 'God for the world in Christ'. But if you begin with 'being', is there any way to the world of time and movement, the historical world where faith takes its rise?[1]

There is no point in building a palace for God to dwell in, in freedom, if his freedom means disconnection from

[1] I have ventured these remarks on Barth's views only with great diffidence. Barth is so clearly part of the main theological picture of our time, and yet he is such a voluminous writer that it is very difficult to pin him down. Thus, at an earlier point in the same half-volume from which I have quoted, in his discussion of 'The Veracity of Man's Knowledge of God' (*Church Dogmatics*, II, 1, p. 243), he is fairly explicit, even categorical, in his denial that 'being' can provide a basis for understanding God. 'In the Bible, however, it is not a being common to God and man which finally and properly establishes and upholds the fellowship between them, but God's grace.' Here Barth bases his opposition to the traditional *analogia entis* on the claim that he does not find it in Scripture. But even so, as we have already seen, Barth is unable to dispense with the conception of being. Not only does he refer everything, including the 'guarantee' for faith and grace, back to the innermost being of God in the intra-trinitarian reality, but he also, in dependence upon Anselm, retains the *aseitas* of God (cf. op. cit., p. 302 f.). At this point, it is true, Barth is thinking primarily of God's freedom, and this is essential to any viable conception of the living God of faith. In other words, the *aseitas* of God is understood in terms of *a* being rather than Being. This may well seem to be more in line with the anthropomorphic and anthropotheistic terms of Scripture. But is aseity an adequate concept for expressing the kind of freedom and separateness which finds expression in the Bible? The discussion is continued in the exegesis of Exodus 3 : 13 f., below.

the world. This freedom is sterile. Nor can it be fructified by talk of God's absolute good pleasure.

Now it is true that the theology of being, that is, the understanding of God as being, has traditionally found one specific point in Scripture where the definition seems to be clearly presented: namely, in the words spoken to Moses at the burning bush.

The words are clearly originative and seminal. They have had immense influence upon the way in which biblical faith has sought for ultimate self-understanding. They have also traditionally been used as the basis for understanding the Johannine words of Jesus, 'Before Abraham was, I am' (John 8: 58), as well as the great series of 'I am' sayings in the same gospel. However, it is not necessary to go into the matter of the alleged New Testament connections of thought. At this point I consider that the exegesis of Rudolf Bultmann indicates the way in which we have to understand the Johannine sayings. In his great commentary on the Gospel according to St John, he writes:

' "Before Abraham was I am." The revealer does not belong like Abraham to the order of creatures that come into being. The ἐγώ which Jesus as the revealer utters is indeed the "I" of the eternal *Logos*, which was in the beginning, the "I" of the eternal God himself. But that the ἐγώ of eternity should come to expression in a historical man who is not yet fifty years old, who, as a man, is one of themselves, with whose father and mother they are acquainted—this the Jews cannot grasp. They cannot understand it because the saying about the "pre-existence" of the revealer can be understood only in faith, for thus only may the proper sense of "pre-existence" be grasped, namely the eternity of the divine Word of revelation. All speculative conceptions of pre-existence which represent Jesus or the Messiah as a pre-existent being that is somewhere available, by that very token subject him to the category of time just as much as the objection of the Jews does in its own way in v. 57. The proper sense of "pre-existence" cuts this kind of thinking right off.'[1]

Let us look, then, at the Exodus passage.

'Then Moses said to God, "If I come to the people of Israel and say to them, 'The God of your fathers has sent me to you', and they ask me, 'What is his name?' what shall I say to them?" God said to Moses, "I AM WHO I AM". And he said, "Say this to the people of Israel, 'I AM has sent me to you'". God also said to Moses, "Say this to the people of Israel, 'The LORD, the God of your fathers, the God of Abraham, the God of Isaac, and the God of Jacob, has sent me to you': this is my name for ever, and thus I am to be remembered throughout all generations".' (Exodus 3: 13-15, RSV.)

Now it is certainly possible to adduce the key words in this passage in favour of the so-called classic theology of God as being. Etienne Gilson speaks in this connection of 'the metaphysic of Exodus'. 'I AM WHO I AM', 'The LORD', and 'I AM' are at least connected by similarity of consonants. YHWH, the divine tetragrammaton, that is to say, suggests the root *hayah*, to be. It is thus not impossible to understand 'I am that I am' as a punning reference to the name Yahweh. But can we go further and say that there is a case for looking upon this whole

[1] *Das Evangelium des Johannes*, Vandenhoek und Ruprecht, Göttingen, 1952, pp. 248 f.

linguistic situation as meaning basically that God, after all, does *not* give his name, but on the contrary withholds it? If this were the final explanation, then the way towards the classic doctrine of God's aseity, his being from, for and of himself, would be unambiguously clear.

Certainly, in the whole passage we must acknowledge that the God whom Moses encounters is in some respects keeping himself to himself. Professor William McKane, in a private communication, has put this point as follows: 'We might be able to agree that the phrase constitutes a refusal of Moses's request. He asks for the name of God to be disclosed to him, and "I am as I am" requires him to enter into a relation with an unnamed God and to accept the uncertainties of such a relation. To know the name of God is to have control of him and this control is actualized in the procedures of the cult . . .'

But there is another, more positive side to the situation which has to be taken into account; and it is this which makes the so-called 'metaphysical' interpretation in the last analysis unsatisfactory. This has been put by Professor McKane as follows:

'Approaching "I am as I am" more positively, we should have to say that it points to the freedom of YHWH or, perhaps, to his transcendence. He is the God who comes to his people when he chooses to come. In so far as the life of his people is open to this coming God (i.e. in so far as they are that kind of community) they will recognize him whenever he comes . . . In so far as they are open to Yahweh their existence will be a historical existence. He is then a God who makes history and who gives his people a history by coming to them . . .'

Here, it seems to me, we have the lines of the exegesis which is most congruent with Israel's self-understanding, and understanding of their history, in relation to their God. Professor von Rad's view is similar and is worth giving fairly extensively:

'The narrative in Exodus 3, a very complex unit both in substance and style, is designed on the one hand to communicate what was new in the revelation of Jahweh—that is, information about the divine name—and, on the other, to show how this new revelation was very closely linked with the history of the patriarchs. Exodus 3 is obviously trying to show the continuity between them . . . Jahweh is identical with the God of the ancestors (Exodus 3 : 6, 13 f.) . . . nothing is farther from what is envisaged in this etymology of the name of Jahweh than a definition of his nature in the sense of a philosophical statement about his being (LXX ἐγώ εἰμι ὁ ὤν)—a suggestion, for example, of his absoluteness, aseity, etc. Such a thing would be altogether out of keeping with the Old Testament. The whole narrative context leads right away to the expectation that Jahweh intends to impart something— but this is not what he is, but what he will show himself to be to Israel . . . the היה is to be understood in the sense of "being present", "being there", and therefore precisely not in the sense of absolute, but of relative and efficacious, being —I will be there (for you). Undoubtedly the paranomastic relative clause adds an indeterminate element to the protasis, with the result that the promise of Jahweh's efficacious presence remains at the same time to some extent illusive and impalpable—this is Jahweh's freedom, which does not commit itself in detail.[1]

[1] Gerhard von Rad, *Old Testament Theology*, Vol. I, Oliver and Boyd, Edinburgh, 1962, p. 180.

I should make only one comment on Professor von Rad's exegesis, which on the whole represents the philologically and theologically acceptable understanding of the whole passage. When he makes a contrast between what God is and what he will show himself to be to Israel, Professor von Rad is not suggesting that what God will show himself to be is a fiction, or in some sense not the true God. On the contrary, by this contrast I understand him to mean that precisely in the way God presents himself, 'will show himself to be', we have the only way in which God's being is accessible: namely, as God's efficacious showing of himself.

The same kind of interpretation may be seen in the exegesis by Martin Buber, which is the more interesting in that, under the influence of Franz Rosenzweig, Buber moved from the somewhat unreflective translation, 'I am that I am', in the first edition of *Ich und Du* in 1923, to an interpretation which is in essentials that of Professor von Rad. The 'ich bin der ich bin' (I am that I am) of the first translation is changed in later editions at two significant points. First, the key words are now translated as 'ich bin da als der ich da bin'—'I am there as I am there'. Secondly, in *Königtum Gottes*, 3rd edition, 1956 (*Kingship of God*, p. 105), he writes:

'*ehye* means . . . to be there with someone, to be present to him, to stand by him . . . God thereby makes no theological statements about His eternity or even his aseity . . .'

Buber's final version for the key words, the traditional

'I am that I am', is 'I shall be there as I Who will always be there'.[1]

Mention of Franz Rosenzweig is not merely a matter of historical interest. Most recently, Bernhard Casper, in a study of the thought of Rosenzweig, Ferdinand Ebner and Martin Buber, has pointed out just how precise and clear Rosenzweig's influence was at this point. Moreover, the point is of immense moment for the development of the dialogical thinking characteristic of all these three thinkers. It is probable, as Fr Casper says, that Schelling was the first to give the words of Exodus the particular turn in the translation when he wrote 'Ich werde seyn, der ich seyn werde' ('I shall be as I shall be'). But it was Rosenzweig who followed out the significance of this kind of translation in his *Stern der Erlösung* (*Star of Redemption*) (1st ed., 1921, 3rd ed., Lambert Schneider, Heidelberg, 1954). In a letter of 2 August 1917 he writes: 'What God is will in eternity be fathomed by no man, yet at all times he will ally himself with us. Or—what is exactly the same—as Raschi interprets the revelation on Horeb, "I am that I am", "I am with you as I was with your fathers"—mere being (das blosse Sein) does not concern men beyond this.'[2]

We have already seen how Metz proposes a similar rendering for the Exodus passage.[3] Walther Eichrodt,

---

[1] *Kingship of God*, Allen and Unwin, London, 1967, p. 105.

[2] Quoted in Bernhard Casper, *Das Dialogische Denken*, Herder, Freiburg, 1967, p. 180. Fr Casper's whole work is an exercise devoted to an examination of the thought of the 'new thought' of Rosenzweig, Ebner and Buber.

[3] See pp. 86 above.

in his large-scale theology of the Old Testament, writes: 'Ich bin der Ich bin, d.h. ich bin wirklich und wahrhaftig da, ich bin bereit zu helfen und zu wirken, wie ich von jeher war' ('I am who I am, that is, I am really and truly there, I am ready to help and to effect, as I have ever been.'[1]

We may now summarize the views of modern Old Testament scholars, Protestant, Catholic and Jewish, as follows: (1) the later philosophy of being is not deducible from the Exodus passage, (2) the name of God is given in terms of his relation to and his historical movement towards his people, and (3) this God 'who makes history and gives his people a history by coming to them' (McKane) is recognized as free, who comes when he chooses to come (yet not out of a primary aseity), and as efficacious, doing what he does as the very making of his people.

These findings are of the utmost importance for our understanding of the being of God. More precisely, we are already in sight of an important finding, which concentrates the whole issue enormously. We cannot yet say that the concept of God's being is meaningless. The temptation to abandon the concept altogether is certainly strong. Ferdinand Ebner, in his highly original personalist thought, which is to be found scattered through a wealth of fragments and aphorisms, as well as in his pioneer work, *Das Wort und die geistigen Realitäten* (Innsbruck, 1922), once spoke of 'the senselessness lurking

[1] *Theologie des Alten Testaments*, I, pp. 116 ff. cf. English translation, *Theology of the Old Testament*, SCM Press, London, 1961, p. 190.

in the little word "is", the senselessness of this idea of a "being" of God in the "third person" '.[1] But at the moment we are not entitled to say more than that the consensus among Old Testament scholars provides a strong basis for an understanding of the God of biblical faith in historical and dynamic terms, and not in conceptions of timeless and static entities, whether eternity or God's aseity. As Eichrodt writes, 'the emphasis lies not on existence at rest, but on active existence'.[2]

Eichrodt is using the word 'existence', rather than 'being', in what seems to be an unwitting departure from the traditional ontological reference which has been found in this Exodus passage. His words sum up the other possibility, not only for this passage, but also for the whole biblical way of talking of God.

This way of talking of God is not, however, very easy to define. It might be called an anthropomorphic way. But this does not say very much, since in a sense even the most exalted transcendence is still somehow attached to man and to human formulations. If we call it a personal way of talking of God, we have again not said very much, until, that is to say, we have succeeded in defining what we mean by personal.

A fuller discussion of this point must await our discussion of what is meant by historical, in relation both to man and to God. Meantime, we may note that, even if talk of God as being is not easily deducible from even

[1] Op. cit., ed. of 1952, Vienna, p. 217.
[2] Op. cit., pp. 118 f.

this classic Exodus terminology, nevertheless, the question whether God may not in some sense be described as *a* being is still not clearly settled.

It is true that this suggestion comes up against strong resistance, and we have already noted that there is a strong tendency among modern theologians to discard this possibility out of hand. So far, at least, as the concept of God as *a* being implies that God is an entity among other entities within the world, we may agree with the resistance to this view. Paul Tillich, aided and abetted by John Robinson, has certainly made this point clear. God is other than all entities within the world: he is the ground of all being. Whereas, if God is understood as a being, then, in Tillich's words, 'he is subject to the categories of finitude, especially to space and substance. Even if he is called the "highest being", in the sense of the "most perfect" and the "most powerful" being, this situation is not changed. When applied to God, super-latives become diminutives. They place him on the level of other beings while elevating him above all of them.'[1]

But Tillich himself is aware of the deep antinomy which confronts us here. Especially in his short book, *Biblical Religion and the Search for Ultimate Reality*, he seems to me to have posed the problem which faces him (and indeed all theology) with unexampled honesty. But he has not solved the problem. Thus, while he cannot help acknowledging the weight of the biblical personalist

[1] Paul Tillich, *Systematic Theology*, Vol. I, University of Chicago Press, 1951, p. 235, and Nisbet, London, 1953, p. 261.

understanding of God, he nevertheless wants to draw the whole mass of problems into order under the one rubric of Being or Being-itself. Thus he writes:

'The dangerous consequence of biblical personalism (viz. in making God less than what *is*) . . . God who is *a* being is transcended by the God who is Being-itself, the ground and abyss of every being. And the God who is *a* person is transcended by the God who is the Personal-Itself, the ground and abyss of every person . . . Being includes personal being; it does not deny it . . . Religiously speaking, this means that our encounter with the God who is a person includes the encounter with the God who is the ground of everything personal and as such is not *a* person. Religious experience . . . exhibits a deep feeling for the tension between the personal and the nonpersonal element in the encounter between God and man. The Old and the New Testaments have the astonishing power to speak of the presence of the divine in such a way that the I-Thou character of the relation never darkens the transpersonal power and mystery of the divine, and vice versa.'[1]

We shall have to return to the question whether the model of the personal is viable for our talk about God. Here we have simply to ask whether Tillich's powerful attempt to bring everything—God conceived as personal, as well as man in his world—under the ultimate category of Being, adds anything, in principle, to the traditional Thomist view. I do not think that it does. It is a modern re-statement of a theology of being which has much to commend it. Especially noteworthy and praiseworthy is

[1] *Biblical Religion and the Search for Ultimate Reality*, Nisbet, London, 1955, pp. 82 ff.

the effort Tillich makes to realize, to make present to himself and to his readers the reality of, man's own experience, including that experience which he calls 'biblical faith'. He does not lose sight of the tension between the personal and the nonpersonal element in religious experience. And he derives the symbols for describing God's life from the concrete situations of man's life. This is possible for Tillich because he holds to the ultimate faith in God's unconditional participation in human life: for this reason the use of human symbols for describing God is both possible and reliable.

But for all that—though we may recognize the justness of Tillich's attempt to prevent all religious experience being subsumed under the category of personal, at the expense of being, and though we may applaud his profound sense of the significance and the necessity of human symbols for describing God—the end of Tillich's theology is not far removed from a certain kind of worldly mysticism in which everything—God, man and the world—is flattened and submerged. For the participation of which Tillich speaks points in the end to an ultimacy in which, as he says, 'the polarities of being disappear in the ground of being, in being-itself'.[1]

One may say, then, that it is by an act of violence— violence to his own biblical faith—that Tillich resolves the dilemma. He loses both man and God in the *Ungrund* in which, if he were true to his conclusion, there would be nothing to say. For the *Ungrund* in which the 'polarities of being disappear' is by definition nothing, *nihil*: it is the

[1] *Systematic Theology*, Vol. I, p. 270.

formless void, the unmoving ground, out of which all movement comes. Tillich has rescued the concept of being at the expense of the concept of beings and of any ultimate distinction between beings.

The Christian doctrine of creation is rather obscure, at least in its positive implications. But what it makes quite clear is the negative—the negation of sameness: the Creator and the creatures are not the same. The link connecting them is the grace of the Creator. Creatures are what they are not in virtue of a sameness of being with the Creator, but in virtue of the grace of the Creator. Nevertheless, it is unnecessary to conclude from this that there is no analogy between the Creator and the creatures. If there were no analogy, and even an analogy of being, there could not even be an understanding of grace. Grace is paramount in the creaturely situation, as it is paramount for this very reason in the situation of the Creator. But the paramountcy of grace does not mean the exclusion of a sufficient participation by way of an analogy of being. Grace, to be understood, requires an analogy of being. It is hardly necessary to add that an analogy is always a link indicating difference as well as likeness.

Tillich's is only one effort to rescue the traditional theology of being, though perhaps the most picturesque. There is a noticeable resurgence of philosophical theology, especially in the English-speaking world, which finds it possible, in one form or another, to revitalize a tradition which has in fact never been in real danger of dying. At worst it is a tradition which has tended to be forgotten. Perhaps the most interesting example of this kind of theologizing is that provided by Mr Peter Baelz, especially in his recent *Christian Theology and Metaphysics* (1967). His work is typical of this tradition in so far as he almost instinctively translates his faith-experience into philosophical language, and even into inherited metaphysical categories. Of course he is entitled to do this, and indeed, like everyone who speaks, he *must* do this: he must use language which has been shaped and provided by some kind of thinking (and of aesthetic perception as well). It is somewhat jejune to attempt to write off all metaphysics as irrelevant to Christian faith. (I myself have been guilty of at least giving that impression.) The important thing is to know what you are doing when you are using certain kinds of language. I think Mr Baelz has to be asked whether, in the following sentences taken from his book, he is really aware of the implications, especially of the last sentence:

'When Christians speak of God as the Father of Jesus Christ, what they are saying about God must be understood with reference to Jesus, but the "God" whom they are speaking about is not simply definable in terms of Jesus, the prophet of Nazareth. He is also "the maker of heaven and earth". That is, his being is the source and ground of being.'[1]

The implications of the last sentence, as I see them, are that a certain tradition of philosophical thinking is here

[1] *Christian Theology and Metaphysics*, Lutterworth, London, 1967, p. 142.

imposed upon a religio-historical assertion. The context of Christian talk of God, which includes a confession of God as Father and of him as Maker, is simply not that of a philosophy of being, such as is implied by Mr Baelz. In Carl Michalson's words, 'The Bible . . . does not ask the question of being but of historical meaning and act'.[1] 'In the eschatological faith of the New Testament being cannot qualify history because it is history which qualifies being, giving it its end.'[2] It is not possible to go into all of the so-called 'existentialist' varieties which flourish today. Of the fairly traditionalist variety which Tillich represents, it is enough to make one concluding comment. On the basis of 'being-itself' there is no sufficiently powerful reason why being should not be simply eternally itself, by itself, at rest within itself, and not only needing no creatures—no other beings—for its self-being, but actually not able to make (or if, by a concession to a nominalist view being able to make, yet not able to associate with) those other beings. (Tillich's understanding of 'being-itself' as also possessing 'the character of self-manifestation' alters the conception of being radically.) What kind of being is it that by nature manifests itself? To ameliorate the sharpness of this conception by means of a correlative conception of human concern—'ultimate concern'—is a splendid stroke, in keeping with Tillich's ineradicable humanism: but it alters the situation radically. The way from being-itself to human concern, and reciprocally from human concern to being-itself, is a

[1] Carl Michalson, *Worldly Theology*, p. 105.
[2] Ibid.

way in which the traffic cannot be simply regulated from the side of either being-itself or human concern alone. The paradox of the relation between God and man is even more acute, and elusive of conceptualization, than Tillich allows. Kierkegaard's living sense of the unease or unrest of faith is a surer guide into the heart of the antinomy of the divine-human situation than either a philosophy of being or a sociology of ultimate concern are able to penetrate.

The bleak situation which can be envisaged, if Tillich's 'Being-itself' were for ever without relation to the world and to men, can also be ameliorated by the forcible addition of some such conception as 'holy'. Thus Professor John Macquarrie, who has done much to restore philosophical theology to a position of reasoned assurance in recent times, would like us to accept the definition of God as 'Holy Being', and this means the God with whom we enter into relation.[1]

To put it in his own words, at the conclusion of a study of 'The Language of Being', Professor Macquarrie writes:

'The believer is convinced that Being has revealed itself as such that he cannot withhold the response of worship and commitment, which is the recognition of Being as "God".'[2]

It is interesting to note that Professor Macquarrie prefaces this remark with a reference to the Exodus passage:

[1] *Studies in Christian Existentialism*, SCM Press, London, 1966, p. 95.
[2] Ibid.

'One of the oldest revelations of God is in terms of Being, in that dramatic moment when he is said to have revealed his name to Moses: I AM THAT I AM.'[1]

In his later *Principles of Christian Theology* (1967), Professor Macquarrie builds upon this general philosophical basis, a great deal of which he owes to Heidegger, a careful structure of a theological apprehension of being. There is undoubtedly great strength in the tradition upon which he draws. But whether he speaks of God as Holy Being, or as 'Being, understood as gracious',[2] or as 'letting be',[3] we have a quite simple question which we must ask here: why does the believer, or the theologian, wish to qualify being in this kind of way? And the answer is not really far to seek. He does so because this is what faith teaches him to do. He does so because this is how he understands his faith. We speak of God as holy, as gracious, as giving us life, because through his historical approaches to men we encounter him, in faith, as holy, as gracious and as giving us life.

The suspicion which is bound to interpose itself between this kind of faith and the grandeurs of a philosophical theology based upon the concept of being is whether the two, the faith and the philosophical theology, are really in such strict correlation. Does the faith need this kind of theology in order to understand itself? Is this game worth the candle? What is it we are trying to say, when we call God Being, or Being-itself, or the

[1] Ibid.
[2] *Studies in Christian Existentialism*, p. 11.
[3] *Principles of Christian Theology*, SCM Press, London, 1967, passim.

ground of being, or Holy Being? Surely, we are speaking first and last of the way God comes to us. The key word is 'comes'; not 'is'. Even the 'Being' of which Heidegger speaks is, after all, accessible to us only through 'beings'. We can speak of 'Being' only through our experience of 'beings'.

I have indicated reasons in scriptural exegesis, and in the self-understanding of faith, why 'God as Being' is not a satisfactory category for Christian theology. I have left open, or at least not entirely closed, the question whether after all we may not have to resort to the unfashionable category of God as *a* being. A full criticism, however, of a theology of being can only be properly completed by the presentation of a countervailing interpretation of human existence. This other interpretation cannot depend upon a particular philosophical system, that of being, or, in Heidegger's phrase, 'fundamental ontology'. It has to depend upon our understanding of man's faith in relation to God as he gives himself to man. To quote from the posthumous work of Carl Michalson:

'New Testament faith is eschatological and not ontological. That is, it is an *answer* to the question of the meaning of history where the answer is given within history *as* history and not at the horizon of history as "Being itself". Even if "Being itself" were identical with God, one would have to say that the New Testament is not oriented to God in his Being but God in his act of self-revelation, God giving history its end in the form of Jesus of Nazareth.'[1]

[1] Carl Michalson, *Worldly Theology*, p. 105.

To this empirical task, then, of understanding man's faith in relation to God as he gives himself to us in history, we must now turn. We may find some help from an analysis of the model of man as historical.

CHAPTER FOUR

Man as Historical

I wish now to examine what I have called the model of man as historical. That is, in terms of the experience of Christian faith, what I wish to do is to present an understanding of this faith in relation to God as he gives himself to man. This relation to God is man's relation to God, of course, and it might seem that the grandeur, the objectivity and the solidity of a theology of being is being replaced by a study of what is 'merely' human. I hope to show that nevertheless along this way we will find ourselves driven to a conception of man which can only be satisfactorily and comprehensively presented in terms of something more than man. As I said earlier (Chapter 2 *ad fin.*), the doctrine of man provides the means of understanding the doctrine of God. I should now like to put this even more strongly: the understanding of man is the only way we have of understanding God.

The approach we must make is, however, not simply anthropological; but it is anthropotheological.

If it be objected that, beginning from man, no way can be constructed which reaches God, then it is not a mere quibble to reply that though indeed a way cannot be constructed, a way can be found: found, because it is there; there, because it is given.

This is grace: grace means the givenness of what we cannot make, and could not even have imagined, let alone desired, for ourselves. Grace is the power which lies for the most part unheeded, and which can only be described in metaphors and heard in the feeble echoes of the might of its passage: it is a new dimension, it is an undeserved gift, it is the 'thereness' of existence, with all its wonderfully subtle and endlessly interwoven textures: dappled light and shade, strength and weakness, joy and sorrow, jest and earnest, need and help: everything contrasting, yet everything uniting, in the variegated harmony of an endless givenness of possibility. All this, and more, is the original givenness of grace, and all that can ever be said in analysis of human experience says nothing if it does not say that, when all is said, everything is grace.

The givenness of everything, which is grace, might seem an odd way of speaking of man. For is the modern human consciousness not precisely a consciousness of man's autonomy, and of his power to make, and even to make himself? The analysis of man which I wish to present will, I hope, make clear in what way we are entitled to speak of man's autonomy and his power to make. At the same time my analysis, proceeding on the basis of this assumption of givenness, will show how man by himself—and that means as an individual self, but also as a self in human community—is an abstraction: the total phenomenon of man, as a concrete historical reality, is more than man. If we dare to call this 'more than man' God, we have of course done no more than indicate our line of advance. Once again, we are up against the immensely arduous task of identifying ultimate reality in such a way that this reality is allowed to be itself.

For we can never completely understand. We can never comprehend the reality of God. An anthropological hermeneutic, such as I wish to use, cannot contain God. The phenomena of human experience are all that we have. They are real, and not a dream. Yet when we are content to rest in the phenomena, we are, paradoxically, ignoring another aspect of the phenomena: namely, the hinterland of mystery in all phenomena.

In this mystery even man is ultimately inexplicable; and in this mystery he is given along with God.

In Luther's words, *scrutator enim maiestatis opprimitur a gloria*. That is, you just cannot scrutinize God: his glory lays you low.

But if man is God's, and is fully himself only with God, then of man too one must say he cannot be scrutinized, for the effulgence of the divine glory which strikes him renders him inaccessible, in the end, to observation.

None of this understanding of mystery is intended to deprive the whole matter of Christian faith of its matter-of-fact, down-to-earth, historical concreteness. We may heartily agree with Professor Ernst Käsemann, when he writes:

'The offence which Jesus occasioned did not consist (as is often babbled) in his posing impenetrable mysteries to our under-standing. Rather, he bears witness to a God who does not correspond to our wishes and views, who breaks our will and also that reason which is influenced by our godless idolatrous will. The free man generates offence because he is only too easy to understand, whereas the sphere of the incomprehensible and mysterious is attractive because it makes ambiguity, arbitrariness and speculation possible, but no genuine offence and no free and joyful certainty.'[1]

For Professor Käsemann, the outlines of Jesus as the free man are clear and hard; and the news of Jesus is good because it is not *simply* attractive, and therefore not attractive in the first instance.

Whatever we may say about the mystery which surrounds both man and God, we must hold by what Professor Käsemann has indicated in his remarks about the nature of the offence in Christianity. We may put it another way: Christianity, whatever else it is, is certainly accessible in the first instance as a piece of history, that is, of human history. Indeed, one may use this basic fact as a criterion for judging some of the things which Christianity has pretended, or has claimed, to be in the course of its history. These can be adjudged as *a priori* impossible because they have abandoned this historical basis. Thus all speculation, all mysteries in the narrower sense of the Hellenistic mysteries and their historical successors, and all metaphysics—again the narrower sense of excogitation starting from an allegedly autonomous enquiring human centre of existence—are *a priori* excluded as not carrying that ballast of historicity which is peculiar to Christianity. For Christianity is not about gods, not even just about

[1] Ernst Käsemann, *Der Ruf der Freiheit*, Mohr, Tübingen, 1968, p. 35.

God. It is not the record of a miraculous epiphany. But it is about man's historical experience.

This does not exclude, as I have already said, the reality of mystery: but this reality is one which can be in a certain sense articulated, as we shall see. Similarly, the exclusion of speculation from Christianity does not mean that we are stranded with mere positivist literalism. Nor is metaphysics in the broader sense of a certain discernible modicum of rationality in the existence of man to be excluded.

For faith is always an understanding faith. Even so-called 'simple faith' has also its rationale, even though it often turns out that simple faith is identical with faith using outmoded forms of understanding. And faith always seeks an ever more coherent understanding of its own reality. It is, therefore, so far from being in opposition to reason that it summons reason to its aid. And of course it also summons to its aid all the powers of judgment and rationality which lie beyond the purview of a reason which is too narrowly conceived as the mere operation of self-knowledge. Or if we say that reason always primarily involves self-knowledge, then we must add that self-knowledge must not be too narrowly conceived. In either case we have to recognize the basic nature of the givenness of man's situation. He is primarily a receiver.

Apropos simple faith, there is a story told by Eusebius:

'It relates the main points of a short controversy between Rhodon and Apelles. Apelles was in some respects in sympathy with Marcion, and in some respects he followed the

older more conservative Christian tradition. He refused therefore to be drawn into the new philosophizing current. And
Rhodon attacked him for his conservativism. He was often
refuted for his errors, which made him say that we ought not
to enquire too closely into doctrine; but that everyone should
remain as he had always believed. He declared that those who
set their hopes on the Crucified One would be saved, if only
they were found in good works. But the most uncertain
thing of all that he said was what he said about God. He had
no doubt that there is One Principle, just as we hold too. But
when I said to him, Tell us how you demonstrate that, or on
what grounds you are able to assert that there is One Principle
. . . he said that he did not know, but that it was his conviction.
When I besought him to tell the truth, he swore that he was
telling the truth, that he did not know *how* there is one
unbegotten God, but that nevertheless that was what he
believed. Then I laughed at him, and denounced him because
he gave himself out to be a teacher, but he didn't know how
to prove what he taught.'[1]

Primarily, knowledge of the self arises in the world,
along with other persons. This has been cogently put by
E. Schillebeeckx, in the essay on 'Faith and Self-Understanding' from which we have already quoted:

'Man sees his inner reality only when he looks out on the
world of men and objects, consequently, only in association
with men in the world. He is only present to himself, only
person, when he is with something else, and especially with
another person. Self-consciousness is then the awareness of a

[1] Edwin Hatch, *The Influence of Greek Ideas and Usages upon the Christian
Church*, Hibbert Lectures (1888), Williams and Norgate, London, 1890,
pp. 135 f.

self-that-is-in-the-world, a consciousness of being with other things and primarily with one's fellowmen.'[1]

I myself should wish to alter the perspective of Fr Schillebeeckx slightly, by saying that human experience, as experience in the world along with others, is primarily historical.

I have occasionally been taken to task for using the word 'historical' in an arbitrary manner. The distinctions which I drew in *Secular Christianity*, distinctions between 'historical' in the sense of past events, regarded as 'facts', and 'historical' in the sense of decisive personal realities, with the conjoined understanding of past history as being realized in the present relation to it—these and other parallel ways of understanding ourselves have not been very appreciatively taken up by many reviewers. Perhaps the characteristic reaction is that by the President Emeritus of Princeton Theological Seminary, Dr John Mackay. Writing in *Christianity Today* for 14 April 1967, he speaks of my book as 'an intellectual symbol of a decline . . .', and he singles out for reprobation the suggestion that we cannot speak of a meaning in history, but can give history a meaning. For Dr Mackay this involves a demythologizing of God as 'the decisive absolute in history' and at the same time the divinizing of man, 'who in becoming a "being for others" becomes thereby the creator and goal of the future'.

Perhaps the key words of Dr Mackay's criticism are that he finds in my view that 'man is solely and absolutely responsible for his own history', 'the sole absolute is "modern man"'.

I should not myself wish to speak of Dr Mackay in such

[1] *The Word in History*, ed. T. Patrick Burke, Collins, London, 1968, p. 43.

terms, of mingled reproach and melancholy, as he uses of me. For I recall vividly the eagerness with which I turned to his writings as a student, and how they seemed to me to lift us out of our narrow churchly and confessional concerns into the wider world which is the true field of Christian faith. It is clear that there is, however, a real barrier between his way of thinking and mine. Perhaps the basic difference is between a normative theology and an utterly radical, utterly self-conscious and utterly free theology. I do not claim by this that Dr Mackay's views are wholly normative, in the sense of being bound by inherited norms, to the exclusion of any whisper of the freedom of the Spirit. Nor on the other hand do I claim that my kind of theology has achieved 'utter' freedom, and the rest. But all the same, the question which animates me is a different one from that which animates the old guard: I am not asking how we may best preserve the outlines of our religious structures, our religion, and its religiosity. This it seems to me is what Dr Mackay is asking when he asks anxious questions about 'evangelism', about the role of the Church, and about the missionary concept. The questions I should ask are those which are relatively untouched by anxiety about the preservation of the structures, and correspondingly touched by the longing for newness, for revolution, for the unpredictable powers of the spirit to engage man in society in ever new ventures of historical existence. Do I mean the spirit with a capital 'S', or 'merely' human spirit? Both.

When I say that human experience is primarily historical, I am excluding two competing ideas: the idea of something outside of history, and the idea of something within history which is able to control history. By the first idea I mean some kind of suprahistory, which is merely the projection of man's understanding of himself on to a screen where the ghostly emanations of his own myth-making are projected. This idea of something 'outside' history, which is supposed to be 'objective', and which in theology usually takes the form of a *Heilsgeschichte* or history of redemption, in fact empties history of its reality. It is the docetic fantasy by which again and again in history, and especially in Christian thought about history, the hard reality is evaded. (I have dealt with this matter more fully in *Secular Christianity*; see especially pp. 110 ff.)

By the second idea I mean all the competing ideologies which are produced by man's own self-awareness, but which like a monstrous progeny endeavour to suppress and control their own author. All the ideologies, including the Christian faith when it degenerates into an ideology, which seek to secure for man a safe and manageable future, are included in this idea. (This matter, too, I have discussed in *Secular Christianity*; see especially pp. 172 ff.)

The first idea tries to deal with history by bringing in a heteronomous power, which is in fact only a wishful selection of man's own powers; the second idea tries to manage history by displacing man himself from the centre of the picture, and establishing some proximate goal—economic, social, religious or aesthetic—as the absolute. Both ideas are based upon a wrong understanding of history. Against them both we say that real history is what happens to us, and moreover happens to us in the daily accessible realm of the interhuman. History is between man and man. It happens; we do not possess it, and cannot control it. It is not an idea, but a demand upon us. It happens to us as a personal task which is to be realized ever anew, in the multiple decisions of our individual life and in the changing circumstances of our public and social existence.

Does this mean that we are fated to live simply in a pluralistic and relativized world? Must we abandon any notion of transcendence? Are the idea of suprahistory, and the idea of an ideology superior to the individual, not precisely of such attractive power because they are able, each in its own way, to offer a transcendental solution to man's question about himself? Am I asking that we should forget such transcendental suggestions as illusory and transfer our aspirations to the living out and the bringing about of a future which is immediately to hand? Is the absolute to be interpreted wholly in terms of man's own powers to choose and to make himself?

This latter view of man, which is properly speaking the secularist view in its purity, is certainly apparent today. This does not mean that it is a view which is actually lived and embodied by a specific group, let alone a majority, in our society. It is much more in keeping with the slow, confused, ambiguous and fumbling manner of expression and of change that such a view should appear in impure, chaotic forms, mixed with relics of outdated views, and in conflict with other vital views of what man is. But if we isolate the characteristics which make for the type of modern secularist man, we suggest that he appears as untouched either by the docetic illusion of suprahistory or by the planning, calculating and manipulative power of an ideological fanaticism. If we try to say what it is positively that characterizes this modern secularist man, then this is by no means easy. Perhaps it is so difficult because he is mainly characterized by negatives: he wants to be left alone, he wants the peace of his own garden, or the peace of the collective, or the peace of the grave. (The death-wish is very strong in modern society, and it is not merely the suicide statistics which have to be adduced as evidence for this: the so-called 'accident' rate on the roads is another piece of evidence, and there is much more besides.)

More positively, however, though still in rather a formal sense, modern secularist man, we may say, lives almost exclusively out of the future which offers itself to him in the form of what is new: new techniques, new planning of society, new enterprises in partnership, in rationalizing and objectifying and computing. The new science of cybernetics is characteristic of our time, in that it is intended to govern and guide human decisions towards the enhancement and advancement of human togetherness, and towards the elimination of sub-human drives.

By contrast with this interest, which is so much a part of the *Zeitgeist* that it is never radically questioned, not merely the suprahistorical dream of an earlier religious and mythological society, but also all the allurements of the political and economic and religious ideologies, are quite superficial. Where modern man is really expressing his basic wishes, we may see how each task or problem which confronts him is no more than the means for a fresh effort towards realizing, or confirming, the intrinsic forward movement and the objectivity of all his social forms.

So far, therefore, as any one tendency may be singled out as the dominant tendency in our society, I should describe it as the readiness of man to live out of the future, in a way that has never happened before. The new, as such, has an almost magical attraction for man.

The place of so-called science fiction in this state of affairs, both as an expression and as a cause of this forward-looking interest, deserves a study for itself. Even though a lot of what is written in this *genre* is just twaddle, and boring twaddle at that, there is other writing which has more to it.

There are the whirling swirling fantasies of Ray Bradbury, especially *The Illustrated Man*, there are the straightforward projections of technical mastery, with a strong allegorical infusion, in the stories of Brian Aldiss, and there are the immensely moving problem stories of James Blish, who has written in *A Case of Conscience* a theological novel which far outstrips the more popular but too preciously mythological stories of C. S. Lewis, *Perelandra*, *That Hideous Strength* and *Out of the Silent Planet*. Lewis's work, in fact, derives from the heraldic and mythological fantasies of Charles Williams, who could do it so much better, and without the overload of conscious virtue which is noticeable in Lewis.

The differences between these masters of the *genre*, however, are so great that it is hard to see the common element. In the stories of *Gulliver's Travels*, or in the period pieces of

Jules Verne, we may the more readily, because of the cruder form, see what it is that gives this kind of story its peculiar quality. I should say that it is the venture into the future which is based solidly on some present and accepted fact. In Jonathan Swift the effect is achieved on several levels at once, as is to be expected of a writer of genius: there is the circumstantial framework, like the reportage of a good newspaper; there are the careful comparisons and main- tenance of temporal and spatial standards. We are *always* aware that in Lilliput Gulliver is a giant and that in Brob- dingnag he is a midget. Of course, Swift made his fame, both in this and his other writings, by his savage critique of society, with its frightening and unrelenting insight into the depths of which men were capable: 'the soul of Rabelais living in a desert', as Coleridge said of him. But on whatever level he is read, Swift is one of the pioneers in the depiction of a self-reliant society, the joke (for to Swift it was a joke) of autonomous man. His description of the computer scientists and cybernetic experts on Laputa is the liveliest stroke of insight into what was on its way, not so far round the corner, in Swift's own day, with its specu- lators and entrepreneurs, as well as the most powerful criticism of the whole world of rationalist achievement.

There is one difference between the writers of earlier generations and those of our own time, in respect of the relationship to the future. The imagination in the writers of our time tends to a certain morbidity and flabbiness; the note of anxiety (*angst*) is struck more frequently, and a fevered atmosphere tends to prevail. We are not far away from mere superstitious concern with fate, in many of the lesser yet tone-setting writers of science fiction. My judgment here is not based on moral grounds, but on aesthetic: a writer who is obsessed with his own dream-life, or with anxious curiosity about the forms of coming society, cannot write with the clarity which is required of all good writing.

Possibly the degraded forms will prevail; which is another way of saying that possibly the autonomy of present-day society will bring about its doom. But there is another hope, and it is that the new, what comes out of the future, may be accepted in a more solid and comprehensive context than that of individual fantasy and *angst*.

This trend for the new, for what can be made, can be seen in the ideas of a sophisticated thinker like Paul van Buren. In this connection I should like to quote some of his less carefully qualified views, as he expressed them in a radio dialogue with myself. He said then:

'I seek to interpret faith in the categories of our pluralistic, relativistic culture of today—I regard the human city as an adequate frame of reference for those who know no other form of life than that lived by speaking human beings. Knowing no other form of life, we are coming to see all things as conditioned by and relative to their context. This is what I have in mind when I speak of our age as secular. A secular faith, therefore, would be one relative to its context, a vision of life and a dream of how things might be that is as human as any other vision and dream. When the category of the ultimate and the unconditioned is no longer in the picture, it is no derogation of faith to say that its vision is conditioned and relative. So, after all, is all that men hold dear, from our finest values to our deepest relationships . . .' The difference (between himself, van Buren, and myself) is that whereas I care for 'the human city in the name of an ultimate unconditioned and transcendent God', he (van Buren) urges us to 'care for the human city in the name of the imaginative view of the city given in the story of your and my household gods and the extent to which you share with all the other inhabitants the life of this great city of human affairs'.[1]

Now here it seems to me that Paul van Buren exemplifies very well one absolutely essential side of our human responsibility. We are called to care for our world as one which is waiting to be made by us. In other words, we must agree that in truth we are summoned to live out of the future. It is scarcely possible to exaggerate either the responsibility or the power of man to do this. Man is entirely responsible, and entirely free, for that which awaits him as a task and a challenge. In this view I am happy to concur with Professor van Buren.[2]

So far as it goes. But this view is not the whole story. For at the same time as we face the future in its myriad possibilities, and choose one of the possible futures by which we wish to be guided, and into which we wish to move, we still remain fully historical beings. Or rather, we *may* remain fully historical. This means that we are at the same time related to what has come out of the past. This relationship in turn affects our understanding of and our relation to the future. The past is not merely past, over and done with, and the future is not merely future, which is somehow to be anticipated and grasped and worked out. But our relationship to the past affects also

[1] From a Third Programme Broadcast of the BBC, 9 November 1966.
[2] I venture to draw the reader's attention to a recent collection of my essays, entitled *The Free Man: Studies in Christian Anthropology*, Collins, London, 1969, which illustrates some aspects of this responsible freedom. The same book has been published in the USA by The Westminster Press under the title, *The Whole Man*.

our understanding of the freedom with which we face the future. For though I agree with Paul van Buren that the vision we may have, in faith, is conditioned and relative, and that our freedom, while thus conditioned, is not controlled by anything else, such as he ascribed to me ('an ultimate unconditioned and transcendent God'): nevertheless, our freedom is not to be understood as the freedom which is simply possible within our conditioned and relativized situation. But our freedom is a paradoxical freedom, and can be expressed only dialectically. It consists essentially in our free giving of ourselves in responsibility, and this means that we freely give in relation to our freely receiving. Our freedom consists in the reciprocity of receiving and giving. Man's freedom can therefore not be defined merely as a multitude of individual possibilities in which each chooses and plans his future (subject only to his particular *Geworfenheit*, the particular context and set of circumstances into which he has been 'thrown'). But man's freedom is a relational possibility and responsibility.

It is on the basis of what I have just called man's 'relational possibility and responsibility' that it is also possible to put new meaning and power into the stale notion of transcendence, what Karl Barth has called 'the tedious magnitude known as transcendence'.[1]

But however tedious transcendence may have become for Barth—and, I confess, in its traditional formulations understandably tedious—we certainly cannot relinquish

[1] Karl Barth, *Church Dogmatics*, III. 4, T. and T. Clark, Edinburgh, 1961, p. 479.

the concept without a real effort to assess its value for us today.

This value, it seems to me, consists in the first instance in the historical actuality of the *experience* of transcendence. Transcendence is primarily something given in our human experience. As a primary 'given' of experience, of course, it is something more than a product of excogitation, but at the same time it appears, it presents itself, as a reality which can be understood and thus presented as an objective idea. The objectivity of the idea, however, which can be recognized in a nexus of things and events, is not primary. It is rather 'secondary objectivity'—and here I use the phrase in the sense proposed for it by Mr Peter Baelz when he distinguishes between this 'objective' knowledge and what he calls 'the primary objectivity in which the other is "given" '.[1] It may be unnecessary to cavil at the description of the other as given in primary objectivity, though I personally should prefer to say that all objectivity is secondary, and that the primary human experience of the presence of the other is the experience of subject with subject which cannot be adequately contained within the description of objects.

Now it is a perfectly reasonable criticism that a description of the other should not be allowed to vanish in a cloud of talk about 'the lived present' or the like. Martin Buber once wrote that 'it is not necessary to know something about God in order really to believe in

[1] See his perceptive study of the interrelationships between theology and philosophy, in *Christian Theology and Metaphysics*, Lutterworth, London, 1967, pp. 104 ff.

Him',[1] and the strictures of a sensible philosopher like
H. D. Lewis[2] are certainly necessary. Jürgen Moltmann
has made a more general criticism of what he calls a
'Seinsmystik der gelebten Gegenwart'—a 'being-mysti-
cism of the lived present'—and, though he does not say
so, I suspect that he is referring to the same kind of thing,
that is, to the *Lebensphilosophie* of which Buber was
certainly one of the products, even if he has to be regarded
as more than just that.[3] The same sort of criticism must
be levelled against the late Professor John Baillie's remarks
about presence, which for him is in the end capable of
being a substitute for faith. The title of his posthumous
Gifford Lectures, *The Sense of the Presence of God*, puts
succinctly the mode of reality which in the end meant
most for Professor Baillie. In his earlier and more discursive work, *Our Knowledge of God*, he speaks of God
as 'the One who is directly known in his approach to the
human soul. He is not an inference, but a Presence.'[4]
In the same book he elaborates a view of God's 'directness
in indirectness' which is intended to obviate the charge
that he is indulging in a kind of obscurantist mysticism.
Yet I cannot help thinking that, as is so often the case,
the theologian is returning to his origins, and that here
Professor Baillie is simply trying to find good reasons for
a conviction which he had somehow acquired from his

[1] *Eclipse of God*, Harper, New York, 1952, p. 40.
[2] *Philosophy of Religion*, The English Universities Press, London, 1965,
pp. 206 f.
[3] Jürgen Moltmann, *Theologie der Hoffnung*, Kaiser Verlag, Munich,
1964, p. 25 (English translation, *Theology of Hope*, SCM Press, London,
1967, p. 30).   [4] p. 126.

earliest days in the Scottish Highland manse where he grew up. For all his air of rational caution, John Baillie was a Celtic mystic, at heart perhaps even a little fey, and while we may agree with him that God cannot be expressed simply as an inference, we must question whether the experience of the presence of the other, which is the core of all talk about transcendence, is adequately expressed as 'directness'—even when this is qualified as 'directness in indirectness'.

The experience of the presence of the other demands a much more cautious analysis. The otherness of the other person, who rises up in my present situation, steps forward and confronts me, is in the first place simply to be described as an event. It happens to me, as an event of our common humanity: it is not just my own idea, and it is not just as an object of my observation and under-standing that I experience the other. In fact, the otherness of the other cannot be conceptually comprehended by me, even though I may extract from the experience a whole inventory of comprehensible and objectifiable data about the other.

If we speak of an event as the primary experience, we indicate that the reality is more complex, and also more unified, than the break-up into two parts, the I and the other, might lead us to suppose. For the reality is not I and the other, but rather we share in a situation which could be described as 'I-with-the-other-in-a-world'.

(This does not rule out the problem of how we perceive

the real existence of others. But it puts this problem in a secondary place.)

The experience of the other is therefore not a problem either of epistemology or of ontology. But it is this givenness of 'I-with-the-other-in-a-world' which determines how we are to describe the experience.

I call it a historical experience. In the term 'historical' are included the elements of time, space, personal existences and a world composed of all these in relation.

Franz Rosenzweig held that we need time and the other in order to be.[1]

While the relation with the other is clearly expressible in terms of subjectivity—that is, of intersubjectivity, of a subject-to-subject relationship—it does not appear that this is the clearest way to express the matter. For the event we are trying to understand is not simply the coming about of a relationship between two subjects, whether in casual and temporary or more permanent connection. Rather, it is to be seen as the disclosure of a reality in which I and the other share.

The relation between myself and the other indicates, not a merely formal constituent of the possibility of our knowing one another but something more, namely, the reality of communion. This communion, which is the primordial possibility which enables us to be human beings, in turn points to the existence of community. It is I and the other together in time and space who form a world.

[1] cf. Nahum Glatzer, *Franz Rosenzweig: His Life and Thought*, Farrer Strauss and Young, New York, 1953, p. 199.

This community in communion is spirit. Spirit is neither the possession nor the expression of the isolated I; far less can it ever be understood, let alone grasped, as though it were an object lying around in our world. It *is* our world: it is the bond and the strength of human existence. Spirit is the total reality of our humanity.

It should be clear that the experience of transcendence is something nearer than a system of ideas, or an order of being or of value which is as it were superimposed on my life. It is precisely the experience of the other as *presence*, as a fully temporal reality, which makes it necessary to repel any such explanation of its origin. The experience comes to me in the heart of my historical existence.

It comes to me as a call: a call to respond and to be responsible in face of the other.

History is the summary description for this mystery of call and response, of responsible human action.

This event, then, this experienced event of transcendence, is clearly a selected event. Does this mean that a great deal of experience is left out? Does it not mean that we here face a great reduction of what is available?

Of course there is reduction. Our human existence arises precisely out of selection and reduction. Human society consists of choice and decision, and this means that other possibilities and other ways are discarded. Not merely this, but there is a drive towards simplification. The more advanced the society, the simpler its basic principles. This does not mean that it may not also be a highly complex society, that is to say, complex in its products and even in its structures. But basically, out of a high society an immense amount is left out: has even been driven out. We see this beautifully exemplified in the society envisaged and anticipated in faith by the Old Testament prophets. Gods were eliminated; sacrality was purged; religiosity was an object of ridicule. There was really nothing left but the one God and his people, who were real people only to the extent that they were faithful to this God. A very simple state of affairs.

At the same, time the experience I have been describing is not confined to what, under the influence of Martin Buber's terminology, is often crudely described as the I-Thou relation. It must be emphatically stated that so far as Buber's terminology implies an *alternative* between the I-Thou relation and the I-It connection then it is misleading. The selectiveness of the human experience which makes the human world is not selective to the exclusion of the 'It' world.

How far Buber himself, in his well-known writings, of which *I and Thou* is perhaps the best known, though there are later essays and other works which may be more revealing, is responsible for the interpretation of the human world as consisting in its most genuine form of I-Thou relations, to the exclusion of the I-It, is a difficult matter to determine. Professor Michael Theunissen, in a most important essay on 'Buber's Negative Ontology of the Between',[1] and also in an elaborate treatise on the meaning of the other,[2] has devoted con-

[1] 'Bubers negative Ontologie des Zwischen', in *Philosophisches Jahrbuch*, Vol. 71, Pt. 2, Verlag Karl Alber Freiburg, Munich, 1964, pp. 319-330.
[2] *Der Andere*, de Gruyter, Berlin, 1965.

siderable attention to this question. It might seem a matter of merely biographical interest, with respect to Buber's own understanding of the nature of personal relationships. But in fact the question is important in its own right because it is a question of assumptions: what are the underlying assumptions of a view which lays so much stress on the reality of personal relationships? Professor Theunissen, it seems to me, has made out a most persuasive case for the view that Buber has made use of a model of intentionality, beginning with the I, which is in the result unable to get beyond the I. Buber's given is the individual I, and so he can never truly enter into the reality of the relation: the relation is the given, and this can also be expressed as the Word.

Now it is true that Buber again and again speaks in terms which imply the priority of the Word and of Spirit over the separate elements in human experience, of things, of persons and of spiritual realities. 'In the beginning was relation', 'elements of the interpersonal', 'the realm of between', 'interhumanity'—these utterances, one at least of which, '*Zwischenmenschlichkeit*', is a coinage of Buber's, all indicate Buber's plain intention to give full place to the *realm* of interpersonal relations, as he calls it.

Nevertheless, as Professor Theunissen makes clear, when Buber attempts to establish an ontology of 'between' ('*des Zwischen*') he is unable to present a positive structure because he has begun with his 'I'. Whether this 'I' is the 'I' of the I-Thou or the 'I' of the I-It does not alter the fact that in each situation he is presenting an attitude of the I (*eine Haltung*). As Bernhard

Casper writes: 'And even if in later works the word *Haltung* (attitude) gives way to the word *Verhältnis* (connection) which is certainly more apt, this connection, which is basically twofold, is always described from the basis of subjectivity. That is to say, Buber, starting from the I and its connection with the other, attempts to describe experience and encounter. The I utters the primary word I–Thou as well as the primary word I–It. This goes so far that in *I and Thou*, meeting (*Begegnung*) is described as a 'working on the one who confronts us' (*Wirken am Gegenüber*) . . . It is the intention of *I and Thou* to overcome the schema of intentionality. But the phenomenon which is described is basically not the event of reciprocal speech, but the *attitude* of meeting'.[1]

If, as I think, there is considerable evidence for this view, that Buber in effect never leaves his own subjectivity behind, and even when he is attempting to describe the ontology of 'between' he is not really doing more than describing the act of meeting in terms of the I, then it must be concluded that Buber never really succeeds in getting beyond the '*Lebensphilosophie*' of his early writings, such as *Daniel*.

This conclusion can, as I have already hinted, be contested on the basis of the very evidence which can be accumulated from Buber's own writings. After all, an analysis of 'meeting' and of 'experience' in terms of primary *words*, of address and response, and his lifelong witness to what he has called a 'neglected and darkened primordial reality'—namely, the two ways in which man

[1] Bernhard Casper, *Das Dialogische Denken*, Herder, 1967, pp. 295 f.

can be in the world—has been of great importance in our time, in helping towards an understanding of what is going on in such various realms as pedagogics, art criticism, psychology and theology. The spectacle of mass man and mass media, and of propaganda and pretence, has been handled by Buber with a skill and insight which has pioneered a great deal of sociological enquiry.

But it must also be agreed that, in comparison with others who have pioneered dialogical thinking, Buber plays the part rather of a high-grade popularizer, of *haute vulgarisation*, than of creative newness.

It is only possible to reach this kind of conclusion if we are at the same time clear that Buber is in his own right nevertheless one of a great line of thinkers. I should not care to go as far as Fr Casper, who speaks of Buber as being 'in the great Western tradition which reaches back, via Eckhardt and Thomas Aquinas, to Aristotle'.[1]

As against an analysis which begins from the model of intentionality, that is, from the willed intention of the subject, we have to understand the confrontation with the other as more basic still. So far we have not been able to reach beyond negations: this confrontation which is the experience of transcendence is not directness, not mysticism, not my own idea, not any kind of object or timeless idea, not an ideological construct and not simply a picture of the world.

To elaborate for a moment on the last point: the historical existence which we are analysing cannot be tied to any particular picture of the world which may be

[1] Op. cit., p. 300, note 59.

adduced to explain it. We have already seen that the traditionalist theological picture of a world of suprahistory is a mythological imposition. The picture of an immanent goal, on the other hand, superior to individual men and demanding their obedience, is also inadequate: in particular because it omits the basic and primordial experience of the other in present and personal responsibility.

Now pictures of the world are continually being formed; they fall upon our shore like the waves of the sea: with every creative artist or poet a new wave forms, a new picture presents itself for our acceptance. This is of the essence of our temporality, that the shifting figures never cease to cross our line of vision. Every moment we see afresh.

This is the stuff of our temporal existence. Whether we are theist or atheist, religious or political, we experience such continual accessions: but they are provisional and makeshift, and as soon as they make claims which overwhelm our own human historicity—as soon, that is to say, as they put forward pretensions to be themselves the actuality of our human existence—they have to be criticized, fought against, and if necessary expunged as dangers to the essential uniqueness of the historical reality of experienced transcendence.

This unique experience, which makes it possible to define man as a historical animal, is therefore not simply a matter of time, of our temporality. Ferdinand Ebner wrote, in one of his striking aphorisms:

THE DOCTRINE OF GOD

'dass alles Sein Gnade ist—dass alle Gnade des Seins im Wort ist—dass der Mensch vom Wort lebt—dass alles, was ist, durch das Wort ist'.[1]

If we paraphrase this as follows: everything is grace, and grace is in the Word, and man lives from the Word, and everything is by means of the Word—then we have perhaps departed somewhat from Ebner's formulation of grace and the Word in terms of being (*Sein*), but not from the general trend of his thought. For even if Ebner talks of being, he does so entirely, as here, in terms of the Word. We may follow this suggestion up by understanding man's historicity as something that happens, as an event, in the first instance between man and man, something which is describable as an active word or as originating spirit. This is the actual reality of existence, and it has the form of an event of the word or of speech.

One of the criticisms of Buber which is most sharply expressed is to be found in Bernhard Casper's *Das Dialogische Denken*. Here he says:

'That on which Buber's thought concentrates is reality as the inexpressible reality of the between. This reality is spirit. And the primal act of spirit is speech (I, 142). But primal *act*. This means that speech, reality itself being supra-act (*überaktisch*) and only thinkable as the paradoxical unity of action and passion, is always derivative ... and pre-eminently understood on the basis of the speaking I.'[2]

What Casper means is clear: it is that for Buber reality is ultimately and primordially inexpressible: the realm

[1] Ferdinand Ebner, *Gesammelte Schriften,* Vol. II, Vienna, 1954, p. 301.
[2] Op. cit., p. 301.

of the 'between' is basic, not speech which arises in this realm. And this inexpressible reality is spirit.

It is indeed possible to see this tendency in Buber. I think in particular of the essay 'Elements of the Interhuman'. However, it would be misleading to reduce Buber's teaching to the primordial and inexpressible mystical experience which was undoubtedly a strong influence, not only in his earlier writings, but throughout his life. Buber himself, in the little writing entitled *Zwiesprache* (1929), expressly disclaimed the mystic and ecstatic experience as the dominant one for his life.

Certainly, we are entitled to draw the conclusion that spirit, as the reality between man and man, is the inexpressible source of being. Rather, spirit, speech, word and history may all be recognized as ways of indicating reality: the reality, that is to say, of man: for in the first instance we have to ask about reality so far as it is indicated in man's own experience. So we may say that so far as we have gone, man's reality appears as what happens between man and man, and may further be described as the active word, which is identical with originating spirit. And this active word or originating spirit is in no sense a mythologized form, but the actual reality of human existence.

But it would be insufficient to stop there. The temporality and openness of historical existence in the face of the other is not a simple phenomenon of humanity, which can be fully expressed in the analysis I have given it. For this analysis stops short, and so far has been chiefly described in negative terms. Transcendence is what happens to us in the confrontation with the other, not an ideology.

What is it, then, beyond what I have already described as a meeting, a demand and a response, an experience of presence?

It is the reality of the spirit which is here present. It is spirit which is the historical reality of transcendence. But 'spirit' is not just a word for the experience of another person in his authentic existence. It is the word for the community of men with God.

'Where two or three are gathered together in my name, there am I in the midst of them'. These words of Jesus are the summary of the spirit as a historical reality, binding men together in a community which goes beyond men.

I say 'beyond men'. How is this to be understood? Certainly not in any sense which treats the 'beyond' of faith as something given to us without involving us. We may not escape from the problem of our own historicity, our *Geworfenheit*, simply by referring everything to Christ as the dogmatically conceived identity of man with God. We are not presented in the being of Christ with a ready-made scheme, or even a fixed model, for the way in which we are to understand our life and fulfil our obedience. Christ himself cannot be fully understood by means of the thought-forms of the New Testament. There is a certain positivism here, but it is not the positivism of a fixed system of belief. It is rather the positivism which is the very characteristic of our histor-icity: in the figure of Christ we encounter not a settled message or an already defined dogma, but the living exemplar of our possibilities as human beings. We encounter the unexpected and the unimaginable, the presence within history of the consummation of human reality: the reality of spirit which joins to us one another, and to God.

Even if no more were to be said than this, we should already be in touch with the possibilities of human freedom: the freedom, that is, to be ourselves, liberated from the old fears, the old self-enclosedness, the old enemy death.

But there is more. Co-humanity is not the whole framework of experienced transcendence. Jesus as the man for others is a reduced and attenuated description of what we find in the historical encounter with this figure. Certainly, even in this description we may have emerged from the obsession with self, and also from the forgetfulness of self, which are the characteristic marks of the traditional view. And we should not disparage the immense amount of goodwill which can be channelled, by careful attentiveness, into simply enhancing the human and personal element in our human society.[1]

If this were all, even then we should have plenty to do. For the malaise which runs through our modern secularist society can be defined, without much fear of contradiction from any side, as tending towards lack of true humanity. Modern man is an easy prey to ideologies, and so far as he hopes at all his hopes are merely directed towards the establishment of new provisional structures

[1] Cf. also Käsemann, *Der Ruf der Freiheit*, pp. 44 f.

for the enhancement of his provisional existence. And the basic insight of Christian faith has never at its best denied the possibilities even in working towards the improvement of the provisional structures of personal relationships.

But if this were really all, then I think that in the name of the freedom of man Christian faith, and with it any understanding of God, would disappear. It would have to disappear, it would be swallowed up in an ideal of co-humanity, and Christ himself would sink into the past, as a hero of co-humanity, one among many who lived for others. Jesus on his own is a tragic figure. To repeat Hegel's words, 'All that remains is the infinite pain of a loss which forces us into reflection and makes us ask about resurrection.' But no resurrection comes from the kind of asking which sees Jesus simply as one of us.

Man's own freedom, itself a gift of that same faith which sees in Jesus something more than the illustration of co-humanity, would also decay and disappear if that faith were to go. And with the loss of freedom authentic humanity would also disappear. A great deal is at stake here. It can be expressed as the question of transcendence, or the question of the right christology, or the question of the right apprehension of God. Or we may say, quite simply and bluntly, even though sensationally, that what is at stake here is man's history, what he can become.

The strength of the Word as the life-giving Spirit is the central affirmation in the Christian tradition, which is able to lead us to an understanding of this 'something more' which lies between man and man. It is not just the sum of individuals in the totality of their experience of life together. Nor is it a spiritualizing addition or extra to human life. Least of all is it simply to be equated with a realm beyond history. We fail to interpret the dominical words aright—where two or three are gathered together in my name, there am I in the midst of them—if we think of a ghostly or numinous presence (that is mythology), or if we think of a suprahistorical realm (that is mythologizing metaphysics). But these words point us to the central reality of spirit as comprehending all co-humanity, and at the same time pointing beyond individual human existence.

Basically, what I am saying is quite simple: it is that man in his historicity is properly disclosed in Christian faith. It is the unique and signal achievement of Christian theology to affirm man in his authentic life as a free and responsible person. This affirmation, moreover, does not abstract from man's historicity: it is in his togetherness with others that he is truly himself. And further, this togetherness is based upon an understanding and acceptance of the Word as constitutive of man's humanity. His temporality is both safeguarded and affirmed as the very way in which he is able to hold together the reality of the past with the hope of the future. This Word is now the subject of our questioning. In what way are we to understand the Word as being related to the historical Jesus? In what way as identical with God? In what way as being the all-inclusive Spirit, identical with both Father and Son?

I ask 'in what way?' For the real question is not *what* Jesus is, or *what* the Spirit is, or *what* God the Father is: but the question is *how* we are to understand ourselves in relation to the realities indicated by these names. If we can begin to understand in what way we may accept our own history, we shall be on the way. And the Christian faith does not really propose more than a way for us to walk.

CHAPTER FIVE

The Historicity of God

I have spoken of the historicity of man, of man as historical and nothing but historical. This I expressed in terms of co-humanity and also of transcendence. But I also spoke of interhumanity. For man's co-humanity is not an adequate conception for the reality of the spirit and the freedom which the spirit gives. In other words, I wished to make a distinction between simple co-humanity and that which is indicated as lying beyond co-humanity. Man's co-humanity points beyond itself. It is not exhausted in the simple confrontation of one with another. But precisely the otherness of the other indicates, and involves, a realm between man and man, and this realm I called (following Buber) the interhuman. This is the realm of man's eminent humanity, it is the realm of the spirit. Here man's humanity is recognized as involving both a gift and a responsibility, a reciprocity and mutuality of action, which in turn indicate a movement of participation. Man's humanity is thus preeminently not a collection of ideas, nor even a repository of affections or feelings: but it is a movement and an action, a doing of the truth in the spirit.

Now this spirit does not mean a spiritualist extra or addendum to man's life, but it is the fulness of his very historicity. Spirit is also historical; it is the pre-eminent historical reality of man's life. At the same time spirit transcends both the individual man and his co-humanity. It does this, certainly, always as historical event. For spirit is what happens to man when he is open to the full possibilities of his togetherness with others. When I say that spirit is what happens to man, I do not mean that the reality of spirit is merely an extension of man's togetherness with others. Spirit is neither an *extra* added to man's life with man; nor is it an *extension* of man's life with man. But spirit is the historical event which transcends man's individual and his communal historicity, and completes it.

At the same time, spirit can only be apprehended within man's historical situation. That is to say, it is only apprehensible within the historical togetherness of faith.

Further, the pre-eminent historicity of spirit is, as it were, both illustrated and confirmed within the entirely historical presence of the eschatological message concerning Christ, that is to say, in every authentic movement of human encounter in responsibility and freedom. And all this now points to the affirmation that this reality of spirit, which we encounter in our faith-relation to this eschatological message, is God.

Does this mean that we may only speak of God in terms of his historical presence? And if so, does this further mean that God is simply historical? And if so, does this mean that he can only be regarded as encapsulated within history? And if so, does this mean that history is a more comprehensive reality than God?

These are the questions which arise out of a consideration of the historicity of man, and it is with these questions that we must concern ourselves now. Our starting-point, as I think, is at least a possible and therefore a legitimate one: that is to say, we start with man, and through a consideration of tradition and of history we have reached a point where we may say that man is not man by himself, that he is not even himself simply as an active and responsible member of even the most comprehensive human community, but that in his very humanity man points beyond himself. We may say that by starting with man we have discovered that man is a question to himself, which is still awaiting an answer.

It is at this point that we face the long and stubborn tradition of theological philosophizing, which is indeed older than Christianity, and which seeks to express the reality of God in terms of being. It is an honourable tradition, and I do not think we can make an absolute break with it. Nevertheless, the demands and questions addressed to us out of the specifically Christian events— and by that I mean in particular what we receive, involved in this older tradition and expressed in the amalgam of thought-forms peculiar to this tradition, of the specific message concerning Christ—point to another way. Basically, it is a way which does not attempt to express God, but rather to address him.

This other way seeks to express the otherness of God

in terms of his historical being-for-men. That is to say, this expression of God's otherness is not a direct expression, but is a response to him in our historical situation. Similarly, even the response or the address cannot be direct, but is made always in faith within the possibilities and responsibilities given to us.

Our inherited tradition of theological philosophizing, on the other hand, tends to locate God as the climax of a philosophical system, or as the conclusion of an argument designed to prove his existence. Along such lines God can never be more than a thing within the world, or a speculative extension of the world. The fatal flaw in this tradition is that God is simultaneously postulated by the human reason, working on its own materials, derived from itself, *and* conceived of as being absolutely for himself. This is a contradiction which staggers the reason. We are asked to maintain at one and the same time that God can be known as what he is for himself, and also that God is derivable from our reflection. The elaboration of this twofold assertion can only be along mythological lines, in which the connection between the God for himself and human experience is displayed by a doctrine of interference on the part of this God in this empirical world. The web of causal connections is broken from time to time by specific acts which are described as miracles.

The very conception of being breaks down as soon as the connection of this God with man is envisaged. Being can then only be expressed as *a* being, and we are back again within the things and objects available to us in our human reflection. For a God who is at once unimaginable and outside history, and yet from time to time breaks into the human world, proposes in the last analysis a conception of God simply as a being alongside the beings in the world.

The traditional supernaturalistic theism which has rectified this dualistic view is therefore able neither to sustain the notion of God as being-for-himself, nor to express adequately the reality of God's connection with the historical world. The in-itself-important insight of the entire otherness of God has been transformed into an ontological speculation.

Such speculation has the laudable intention of rising above the evanescence of human history. It wishes to reach something permanent and enduring. But it succeeds only in positing either a completely immobile and static conception of being from which there is no way into history, or a separate being which is only separate by courtesy of human conceptions of being. Essentially, this God is either posited as incomprehensibly inactive, with sporadic bouts of activity, or as enclosed within the world, at our disposal. In either case, this God is for ever imprisoned within a particular human conceptuality.

But, you may object, what other way of talking about God can there possibly be? Are we not bound necessarily to our own conceptuality? And are we not therefore faced with just two alternatives? Either we postulate God as outside the world or we assimilate him to the world. And if, as I say, we postulate God as outside the world, then there is no way of overcoming the separation. God is wholly other, and the world is left to itself. But is the other alternative not even more calamitous? Namely, the alternative of finding him only in the world? Are we not then reduced to an even more relativized anthropomorphism than that which we are able to produce by a rational exploration of the concept of being? Is it not better to secure God as *causa sui*, or *prima causa*, than to have him reduced to an expression of man's own experience within the world?

In contemporary theology there is indeed a tendency to take the risk of embedding God entirely within humanity. It appears strikingly in those American theologians whom I mentioned earlier. Paul van Buren's answer to the question, What meaning may we ascribe to the word God? is short and simple: The word is now meaningless, and we would do better not to use it.

For van Buren this assertion contains both a negative and a positive element. The negative element is one which he shares, as he says, with Bultmann, namely, that 'the whole tenor of thought of our world today makes the biblical and classical formulations of this gospel unintelligible'.[1] In regard to the whole patristic effort to formulate a satisfactory christology, he says, 'If they (the patristic theologians) had been more consistent in saying that God is unknown apart from his self-revelation and that we must begin with Jesus Christ in order to know anything about God at all, they might have been able to begin with the cross as the event of self-revelation of a God who is quite able to take suffering to himself and

[1] *The Secular Meaning of the Gospel*, SCM Press, 1963, p. 6.

whose glory is so great that he can also humble himself'.[1]
Here we see the positive element in van Buren's view,
which he develops in his analysis of the kerygma: there
is for van Buren a historical reality in the story of the
man Jesus.

His whole position, however, both negative and
positive, is controlled by his acceptance of what he calls
the modified verification principle of the analytic philosophers. The original claim of the logical positivists was
that 'apart from the assertions of logic and mathematics,
only statements which can be verified or falsified empirically are meaningful'.[2] So statements about God or
transcendence and the like, and indeed the whole body
of classical metaphysics, could neither be proved nor
disproved: strictly speaking they were meaningless. But
in contemporary linguistic analysis there has been a modi-
fication of this principle. This analysis now asks what
kind of things would count *for* an assertion and what kind
would count *against* it. And the assertion or statement
has to be looked at in the way it functions in actual use.
The meaning of a word or statement is in fact identical
with its use.[3] More account is taken of the *Sitz-im-Leben*
of the various forms of language. Van Buren makes a very
sharp distinction between what he calls cognitive and
non-cognitive propositions. Only propositions which can
be empirically verified are cognitive. Propositions about
God are non-cognitive, that is, they merely indicate a

[1] Ibid., p. 42. [2] Ibid., p. 15.
[3] L. Wittgenstein, *Philosophical Investigations*, Blackwell, Oxford, 1958,
§ 43.

THE DOCTRINE OF GOD

perspective, or what R. M. Hare has called a Blik: they are not public and objective: they say nothing about a reality that is independent of the speaker's or the believer's attitude. That is to say, to speak of God is merely a roundabout way of speaking of man.

You will notice that in this distinction between cognitive and non-cognitive propositions van Buren has in fact fallen back into the earlier intransigent position of the logical positivists, and is not as flexible and open here as the analytical philosophers who expressly speak of various 'language-games' and of the way words and statements actually function in their use in language. For van Buren all that is left is the human perspective, in which 'statements of faith are to be interpreted . . . as statements which express, describe or commend a particular way of seeing the world, other men and oneself, and the way of life appropriate to such a perspective'.[1] And this particular attitude is derived from the Christian norm, which he describes as 'the series of events to which the New Testament documents testify, centering in the life, death and resurrection of Jesus of Nazareth'.[2]

What we face here is an immense reduction. For the gospel is simply regarded as the story of the free man Jesus, who has set his disciples free. There is certainly something here which is positive, simple, and even attractive: the picture of a man who is truly free, free from anxiety and free for others—a man whose freedom is infectious for us, even in our time.

But can such a simple christology, in which the trans-

[1] Op. cit., p. 156.   [2] Ibid.

cendence of God becomes merely a perspective and a wholesome infection, bear the weight and contain the depth of the dialectic of man's history with Christ? Certainly van Buren has attained freedom from the dead weight of classical Christian metaphysics. But in its place we have a christological positivism resting on a naïve and crude hermeneutic. For example, he says, with reference to John 14: 9, 'He that hath seen me hath seen the Father', 'Since there is no "Father" to be found apart from him, and since his "Father" can only be found in him, the New Testament (and this passage specifically) gives its answer to the question about "God" by pointing to the man Jesus. Whatever men were looking for in looking for "God" is to be found by finding Jesus of Nazareth.'[1]

Thus the word 'God' becomes superfluous and God himself is buried in history. But in this perspective history is no longer history, for it has lost the dimension of transcendence which distinguishes it from mere happening.

Thomas J. J. Altizer is even more explicit. In a key sentence he says: 'If there is one clear portal to the twentieth century, it is a passage through the death of God, the collapse of any meaning or reality lying beyond the newly discovered radical immanence of modern man, an immanence dissolving even the memory or the shadow of transcendence.'[2] In these circumstances Altizer sees only two possibilities. We can either re-entrench our-

[1] Ibid., p. 147.
[2] *The Gospel of Christian Atheism*, The Westminster Press, Philadelphia, 1966; Collins, 1967, p. 22.

THE DOCTRINE OF GOD

selves in the established forms of Church tradition, or else we must affirm the death of God and look for a purely secular presence of Christ in the world. He sees the first possibility as a kind of gnosticism which isolates the content of theology from human historical existence. The other possibility, the present-day radical affirmation of a world without transcendence, he sees as bringing together the fragmented elements of historical culture into a significant unity. Nietzsche, Blake, Hegel are all drawn upon as well as the thought-forms of oriental mysticism, especially Buddhism. Nevertheless, he tries to bring all these eclectic influences under the rubric of Christ as the Word made flesh. In that respect we must concede that this is still Christian theology.

Christ, the Word made flesh, signifies for Altizer the historical death of God. This is kenotic theology developed to a point where it becomes transformed. The older kenotic theology taught that in Christ the divine attributes were laid aside. In Altizer's kenoticism God empties himself altogether in Christ. And so the death of God in Jesus Christ is for him something absolute. Since the death of Christ there is no exalted Lord above us any more. Transcendence is wholly transformed in Christ. In him the strange majesty of God becomes a forward-moving actuality within human life and human experience. 'It is precisely because the movement of the Incarnation has now become manifest in every human hand and face, dissolving even the memory of God's original transcendent life and redemptive power, that there can no longer be either a truly contemporary movement to transcendence or an active and living faith in the transcendent God'.[1]

Our attitude to such a theology cannot be unambiguous. It exposes the hopelessness of all attempts to preserve our vision of the transcendence of God by merely reaffirming the concepts of a bygone age. God is not an idea nor is he inseparably bound to any idea. It recognizes that the Christian faith centres on the historicity of God in Jesus Christ. It is within human history that we know and adore and serve him. It is this profane world and no other which is his world.

But, in the heat of the moment, does such a theology not mistake a valid protest and a lively insight for the final answer? Does it not make the action of God fit too comfortably and readily into the ideas and moods which lie ready to hand in our contemporary culture? Just as the transcendence of God cannot be encapsulated and preserved within the conceptuality of a past age, so also can it not be exhausted in our own historical perspective. What I miss most here is that distinctively Christian understanding of history which ascribes a full, positive meaning to the past, yet nevertheless does not see that meaning as exhausted within the historical process. The paradoxical identity of historical happenedness with an eschatological fulfilment is not to be found in Altizer. When history is understood as a self-enclosed process and nothing more, then we are held fast within an immanentism which leaves no room for the givenness of our life and the world and for the grace of what is given.

[1] Op. cit., p. 136.

We can see similar tendencies to take the risk of embedding God entirely within humanity in certain aspects of German theology today. Herbert Braun does not seem to me to be far away from Paul van Buren in this respect. In various essays he has expressed his special concern, which arises out of his New Testament work, to oppose a theism bound to a particular world-view.

In 'The Problems of a Theology of the New Testament'[1] Braun writes:

'There is no denying that God and his world are *also* looked upon as an object, a thing. But I think I have shown . . . that such objectification is not in line with the real trend of the New Testament. But as what, then, is God to be comprehended?

'Certainly not as the one existing for himself, not as a species which can be comprehended by only this term. Rather we must call God the Whence of my being driven around. And my being driven around is determined by the "I may" and "I shall"; it is determined by being sheltered, and by duty. Shelter and duty are not given to me, however, from out of the universe, but from the other, from my neighbour . . .

'God is the Whence of my being sheltered by, and having a duty towards, my neighbour. Hence to remain in God means to remain in the concrete act of turning towards my neighbour: he who remains in *agape* remains in God (I John 4: 16). I can only speak of God in speaking of man; that is, anthropologically . . . God is implicit in man as man, man in his co-humanity . . . So God is a certain kind of co-humanity.'

Braun's intention is clearly to prevent a too easy identi-

---

[1] *Zeitschrift für Theologie und Kirche*, Beiheft 2, Sept. 1961, p. 17.

fication of a picture of God or a thought about God with the historical reality of our engagement with God, our encounter with him, in and through the demands addressed to us in our history. With this intention I thoroughly sympathize. It is in line with what I have already said about the historicity, the freedom and the responsibility of man in his co-humanity. But we still have a real problem on our hands, and it is brought out clearly in an essay by Johannes Körner.[1] There Körner speaks of the necessity for thinking through the divinity of Christ more consistently, 'as from the historical reality of Jesus Christ'. And he goes on: '. . . the testimony to Jesus Christ in the New Testament: is God.' However, 'the word "God" and the subject-matter "God" have by no means become redundant. It is indispensable as the predicate of Jesus Christ, in order to express his significance and the reason for our faith in him. Only we must be sure what we mean by the predicate "God", over against theism: it is man and history in a relation of transcendence . . . In the Christian proclamation "God" is never a merely formal existential, but at the same time always expresses the person of Jesus Christ . . . In this context, "God" remains to a certain extent . . . an abstraction; speech about him belongs to the realm of saga and myth without which neither theology and proclamation nor indeed any statement related to existence can do, and of which it need not be ashamed.'

In other words, what Körner does is to emphasize the co-humanity in such a way that only Christ is left: in

[1] *Zeitschrift für Theologie und Kirche*, Dec. 1966, especially pp. 486 f.

order to save appearances God is still spoken of, certainly not in terms of being, but simply in terms of saga and myth. This seems to me to be a policy of despair. Better than this would be an absolute silence concerning the God who can certainly not be described simply as a mythologized abstraction.

A more consistent effort to present a new philosophical theism is to be found in the work of Schubert Ogden. In his book *The Reality of God* he, too, speaks of God's absoluteness as an abstraction.[1] His words are 'the new view construes God's absoluteness as simply the abstract structure or identifying principle of his eminent relativity' (p. 65). By relativity Ogden means the eminent related-ness of God to all other being, that is, to 'the whole universe of nondivine beings, with each one of which his relation is unsurpassably immediate and direct' (p. 60). There is a real effort of thought on Ogden's part to bypass the traditional theism. But the consequence of his view, however carefully he tries to guard it by speaking of God as absolute, is that God as the supremely relative Self or Thou is conceived of as becoming. God is involved in a process of 'self-creation' (p. 64), and this self-creation is tied up with human history. This view has the merit of conceiving God basically in terms of historicity. In fact, for Ogden it is only in the reality of human historicity that God may be concretely identified. But the attempt which Ogden makes to ensure to God all the traditional metaphysical attributes as well, by speaking of him as the ground of all relatedness, is not more than an abstraction.

[1] SCM Press, London, 1967.

These attributes do not constitute the whole of God's perfection. But this perfection is 'something unimaginably concrete: (namely) the ever new synthesis into his own everlasting and all-embracing life of all that has been or ever shall be' (p. 61).

This view saves the reality of God at the expense of his completeness. It is a view for which Christian faith must have a great deal of sympathy. For to Christian faith God is not a metaphysical principle, and he is truly involved in human history. And it is only through his actions, through his confrontation of us, that he is accessible. I should therefore agree with Ogden when he says that we must reconceive the traditional attributes 'on the analogical basis provided by our own existence as selves' (p. 61). But precisely this giving by God of himself to man in history makes it impossible for us to draw Ogden's neo-metaphysical conclusion about God. Ogden is forced into a very serious inconsistency when he asks us to accept the reality of God as meaning both the abstract principle of all relatedness and the self-creative activity of God. Certainly, this variation of the process philosophies of Whitehead and of Hartshorne can help us to grasp the significance of human historical becoming; but it cannot also expect to save the absoluteness of God except as a face-saving gesture, or an idle speculation.

Does this mean that we are forced into an even more explicit anti-metaphysical position? Must we say that because God cannot be affirmed directly as the conclusion of a philosophical argument, then he cannot be affirmed in any way that can be reasonably dissociated from the ongoing course of human history itself? Must we take hold of the one horn of Ogden's dilemma—namely, the view of a self-creative God who becomes? If we accept this position, then it follows that we must also concede that there is no difference between affirming God and affirming man. We can call God man, if you like; and we must also call man God. We should then have sunk our differences with high-minded secularists and reached the apotheosis of man.

There is an ambiguity and even a malaise in the modern secularist position. This ambiguity and malaise I should diagnose as being due to an insufficient radicality in secularism itself. Modern secularism is not secular enough. That is to say, it does not take seriously enough the very historicity which is the source and the context of its responsibility. In particular, it tends to replace man himself, man as a free and responsible being, by some cause or ideology towards the achievement or fulfilment of which it is ready to manipulate the future. But this manipulation and anticipation of the future threaten to destroy the very freedom and responsibility which are the source of the powers of secularism.

So we have the paradoxical result that the autonomy of the reason of modern secular man is threatened with engulfment by its own products. And this threat is at the same time a threat to faith. That is, faith which makes man's autonomous responsible action possible, tends in our present situation to become irrelevant. It becomes irrelevant because the question of God disappears from the scene in which secularist man is at work. In general, therefore, we face a situation in modern secularism which is simultaneously a threat to man, to his co-humanity, and to any possibility of giving meaning to the word God. Or, as I have also put it, with the passing of the old metaphysical structure of thought which understood the world as divided into two realms, the natural and the supernatural, the profane and the sacred, the conception of transcendence has become questionable. Whether modern man may be said to be aware of his world as given in any sense, or aware of the numinous, it is I think fair to say that he nevertheless understands himself in terms of his own entirely self-sufficient world. It is an entirely relativized and pluralistic world in which he lives, and its advancement and enhancement lie, on his views, entirely within the empirical realm of the planned choices which are available to him.

As I have indicated, we cannot go back to our traditional ways of thinking about God and man and the world. These ways were in any case an attempt to identify the free responsibility of faith with a normative doctrine or normative doctrines which depended upon a specific world-picture.

You might ask, Why bother to rescue the word God for modern man? Laplace found no need for the hypothesis of God in the natural sciences, and Nietzsche affirmed the death of God as meaning the death, as Heidegger has said, of the God of Greek metaphysic: that is, Nietzsche expressed the fate of two thousand years of European history (cf. Heidegger, *Holzwege*, pp. 193-247). What then is left? What does a man really mean when he says 'God'? The word God, which was originally a name, has become so misused, as a battle-cry, as a symbol for a retreat from historical responsibility, as the conclusion of a philosophical analysis and as the representation of a private pietistic experience, that we might well decide to get along without this name. For through man's arbitrariness and hatefulness the name has become so soiled that it sometimes seems as though it can never again be made clean.

One thing seems to me to be necessary in this context, and that is that we recognize the necessity for silence, or at least for a certain reserve, before we dare to use the name of God. We must not pretend that we can expose the whole mystery of this name. A *theologia negativa* still has a most important part to play. Nor can we hope by our great words to force God out of his hiddenness. We cannot expect that we can bring God to light by means of our little bit of reason or of faith. There are mysteries which can never be solved.

Even in our relation with someone whom we know and love there is a surrounding mystery. The other reveals himself to me as one who is there for me out of his incomprehensible fulness. I cannot grasp this fulness, what we may perhaps call his being-for-himself, but I can only have an inkling of it through what he is for me. In an analogous way we cannot grasp the fulness of God's being, we can only have an inkling of it through what he is for us. We apprehend God in his acts, but we do not comprehend him in his being.

This recognition does not mean that we capitulate

before something that is simply irrational. The believer has his *ratio*, he has his reasons, but they lie in the experience of faith itself.

So we cannot dispense with the attempt to use the name of God. Whatever the difficulties, this is not possible, precisely because we are involved in history and because God himself, God as a Name, comes to us only in and through this history. God is embodied in human history.

So our task must be to lift the Name of God out of the dust again and to set it over the hour of our responsibility.

CHAPTER SIX

The Transcendence of God in History

I said that man in his historicity is properly disclosed in Christian faith. And I also said that the means of understanding the historicity of God is the historicity of man. Man in his togetherness with man, I said, is based upon our understanding and acceptance of the Word as constitutive of man's humanity.

That is to say, man is man in virtue of the Word. What is this Word which is made to carry such a load?

It is easier to say what it is not and what it cannot do than what it is and can do. It is not identical with the conception of a being, as exhaustively expressed in the reality of the Word, which can be recognized as a static, substantial and conceptualized entity. The reality of the Word does not deny the reality of the objective referent: but the reality of the Word is not expressible as a state of affairs between entities. That is to say, we cannot talk here of beings as the primary reality who are then connected by the Word, whether in terms of words or in some other form (e.g. common loyalties, common obedience, common purposes, or the like).

Nor can we stretch our talk of beings in order to reach

Being as the primary reality of which the Word is an expression. The reality of the Word is not dependent upon a prior conception of reality, derived from an idea of Being (which in its turn is approached, as in Heidegger, by means of beings). If this were the way of the Word, then there would be no way of understanding the truth which inheres in the Word except as a conceptual system derived from Being. But what meaning is there in Being which is not put into it by way of man's conceptualizations? For what other way of approaching Being is there save man's own experience, of his own being and of other beings?

So, if we assert that Being is the truth, all we can mean is that men in their introspection and their inter-relationships and their apprehensions have put the truth there. In this area the order of knowing is prior to their order of being, empirically and logically. What meaning, other than our extension of man's own grasp of meaning, can be found in the ontological assertion, the indication of Being itself? But the reality of the Word is not a meaning put into it by men. The reality of the Word is not to be found in such projections—or in the positing of Being, but in the intrinsic power of the Word. For the Word has power to bring about effects.

We may still speak of Being, but the grammar of Being which is most appropriate to the reality of the Word is the language of the first and second person: it is the language of address and response, of man's being addressed and his responding.

If this means that we must speak as J. Macquarrie does

of Holy Being, could this not be more simply and more biblically described as Holy God? Why introduce the awkwardness of 'Being', which you have to give another quality or look to, by adding 'Holy'? Should Occam's razor not work here?

This does not mean the reduction of the reality of the Word simply to that of the so-called personal model. We may recall the criticisms I have also mentioned of the limitations of the person-to-person relationship, especially as in Buber. Of course in one sense the reality which we are trying to indicate is a reality of personal existence. That is, it concerns the total life of men, in their singularity and their possibility. But this totality cannot simply be expressed in terms of human persons and by implication and extension—another version of the *via eminentiae*—in terms of God as a Person. The reality which lies between man and man, and which is simultaneously the indication of or the witness to the reality of God, cannot in the last resort be expressed by the common, reiterated pointing to the Word.

The Word is between man and man, but the Word is not just an It. Nor is it, however, just a Thou. It would be wrong to eliminate the insights brought with the person-model. But it would be misleading to rest the whole meaning of the Word in the person-to-person reality.

For the Word constitutes—i.e. makes possible—the engagement of man with man. The Word is the givenness, the gift, the grace, the apprehended reality of the spirit.

Buber has only hesitatingly grasped the importance of the Word. J. Robinson, likewise in dependence on Buber, clings to the personal 'model'; so far as this goes, it is not wrong; but it does not enter the heart of the givenness which is the Word.

The Word is an event. It is entirely historical. It is not for that reason either submerged in immanence or tethered to a particular metaphysics of transcendence. (Indeed, it might be worth trying to understand the Word without reference to either of these notions . . . ?)

The question which focuses the issue is: how may we speak of God? and the basis for an answer can only be in terms of our experience, that is, anthropologically. But to speak of God in terms of man does not mean either (1) that God is thereby simply a part or an extension of man, or (2) that he is entirely comprehensible, or even addressable, as person. In (1) we still have to reckon with the powers of analogical speech: God-talk arises out of human experience, yet God is not identical with human experience—except in so far as human experience itself also contains a reference to transcendence in the self-existence of the other. In (2) we have to reckon with the powers that are not comprehended in personal existence. Here, however, we face an extreme mystery—though this mystery likewise is indicated in human experience. For in human experience the person-to-person relation is not exhausted in terms of person. On the one hand I-It is a permanent condition of I-Thou and provides objectivity and continuity. On the other hand the person-to-person relation paradoxically is present in its fuller potentiality when the hinterland of the personal relation offers a reality which is not personal. This non-personal reality is spirit, the reality of the between.

This question which has so long tormented me, in what way we may speak of God as personal, and in what way as impersonal (or as Being), may well be the kind of question that admits of no answer. Or it may admit of an answer only by being transposed into a different context. For one thing, God must be regarded as both personal and impersonal—and both together. But beyond that the question of God can be answered only in terms of the questioner and his world. For whatever we try to do to eliminate worldly impurities from our idea of God (and of course we do this), it still remains true that we can speak of God only in terms of human experience. This does not result in sheer anthropomorphism; but certainly it means downright anthropology: God is seen through human eyes: only our human experience is available. Revelation can only take place through human experience.

That is to say, we can know God only as having a history which is involved in our history.

If God is historical, is he subsumed under (the category of) history? Is history not then greater than God? The 'something more' which we believe God to be—how is this to be defined except (a) mythologically (*Heilsgeschichte*-Cullmann) *or* (b) existentially (i.e. historically)? The category of history *must* include God, but it can only include him if he is more than history: but this is (rationally) inconceivable—for how can there be anything more than history? So we have to fall back on (1) *via negativa* and silence, (2) personalism (which is also a mystery), and (3) eschatological faith.

When I say that God is historical I am not including him within history like a spirit in a bottle or a ghost in a machine; but I am including history in God. And history is the only form in which we 'meet' and believe in God.

The notions of inclusion and exclusion do not yield an adequate model.[1]

If the reality of God is historical rather than metaphysical, does this make God subject to change?

Karl Barth, after talking of the constancy and thus the immutability of God, goes on to say: 'There is such a thing as a holy mutability of God. He is above all ages. But above them as their Lord, as the βασιλεὺς τῶν αἰώνων (I Tim. 1: 17), and therefore as the One who— as Master and in His own way—partakes in their alteration, so that there is something corresponding to that alteration in His own essence. His constancy consists in the fact that He is always the same in every change . . . holy mutability . . . (not) unholy mutability'.[2]

Barth however, with all his apparently liberal recognition of the alteration or change in God, speaks in what I suppose he calls a paradoxical way of his not altering his unalterable being. What can this mean except the

---

[1] See especially I John 4. This provides a better model for understanding both the absence and the presence of God. God has never been seen by any man. God dwells in us if we love one another. His love is brought to perfection in us. Here is the proof that we dwell in him and he in us: he has imparted his spirit to us.

[2] *Church Dogmatics*, II. 1, p. 496.

consistency of self-identity which is nevertheless, as historical, changing all the time?

Tennant spoke more clearly when he spoke of God's self-consistency through change. He clearly articulated this as a moral characteristic.

What Barth calls 'mobility and elasticity' in God needs much more careful analysis. Then we must begin to ask how we may really separate God from the world. Of course we already do this and we must: here I agree with Barth (and so with Kierkegaard) that God is 'other'.

The Christian doctrine that God created the world means that the world is recognized as *distinct* from God. There is therefore a sense in which it makes God disappear from the world. The early Christians were called atheists by their pagan opponents. That is, they were seen to be expelling the gods from the world (and evil spirits as well). From this comes the possibility of a world of nature which can be an object of natural science.

From this comes also man's freedom and possibility of growth, since God is believed to be no longer mixed up in the world. The world is de-divinized. There are no more devils and gods mixed up with it. The world goes on its own way, in freedom and autonomy.

It is possible to say that the old Roman civilization died of a metaphysical disease, that is, it had the wrong idea of itself and its possibilities. It made a simple identification of the divine with its own world and its own history.

The difference which Christianity makes is that it guards the freedom of the world for science; and it guards the freedom of man for faith.

In recent theology this withdrawal of God from the world has been forced upon our attention. But we need to distinguish two senses in which he is a disappearing God.

Firstly, certain formerly well-established ways of talking about God are no longer viable. In this respect lots of things should be allowed to go.

Secondly, in his relation to the world he is transcendent. He is qualitatively different. Yet we can only speak of him in terms of the world—that is, in terms of his ambiguous appearance within the world. Here we talk in symbols as we must, and point to a reality which we cannot express, but at the same time we point to a dimension which is real in our own lives.

These two ways of understanding the disappearing God are intertwined. That is, we give up certain ways of talking about God because we recognize the *one* way in which we are able, dimly, to apprehend him.

His disappearance gives room to the world to be itself and man to be himself. This being themselves of the world and of man in turn, when properly seen, point back to God who had left them alone. This is always in danger of becoming the story of the prodigal son: the world and man make the most of their being left alone, and they end up by making the worst of it. Then the autonomy degenerates into an ideology, and the world and man are distorted and lost. The autonomy breaks up into ideologies, and the fulfilment of the autonomy in depth is impossible.

This disintegration of our perception of transcendence

into autonomous ideologies confronts us in the urgent problem of re-uniting scientific integrity with moral responsibility.

The reality of the problem of controlling power, especially the ramifying rampaging power of scientific innovation, and technological advance in every field, is to be seen in the wider context, that is, the context which includes the man who is a scientist as well as the men who are the recipients of his bounty or his terror. In this wider context it is a failure of the scientist as scientist if he refuses to ask what possible use his new powers and gifts might be put to. To avoid the human question, the moral question, about the development of nuclear power, is to be unscientific, unfree, ideological. The only ideology is that of freedom and responsibility—if you can call that an ideology, which I cannot.

The delusion of wholeness, the refusal to recognize openness, characterizes the secularist today. He thinks he is self-sufficient. Does death not come into every balanced picture of life? And the characteristic of death is its power to pick out each person, by himself, and thus to qualify his life's self-sufficiency.

What we all want is duration, lastingness, and we want it in the actual concrete things, experiences, etc., of life: that is, we want duration in the non-durable.

When this turns out to be impossible, or when it seems to be impossible, one of two courses is open to us: either we look for the durable in another way, which has little or no connection with the non-durable; or we abandon any direct wish for durability and concentrate upon the non-durable. Either we turn gnostic or we turn hedonist (Epicurean). But neither way is a truly human way.

The daring nature of Christianity consists, from this angle, in its philosophical stance: it takes the bull of impermanence by the horns and shakes it into permanence. It asserts the permanence of time, of body and of history. (This must also mean that space is permanent—for can you have body or history without space? I doubt it—so here is a fine collection of permanencies!)

But this daring is only rational when we are able to transpose the actualities into another kind. This does not mean that we must be able to produce another rational schema, as it were, to replace the present rational—but not rational enough—schema; it does not mean that we just add the concept of supernature to nature and then conclude we have really said something. But it means something a bit more subtle, something like thinking in another dimension in mathematics. To transpose in music is both the same and different: something of this kind is needed in thinking through the way in which, in Christianity, duration is introduced into the non-durable and, harder still, life into a death-ridden situation.

History, as time, space, body and passingness, is given meaning in terms of this transposition. In terms of this transposition God is rescued in human thought from being swallowed up in the death of Christ.

If some such effort is not made, then we shall find ourselves in the position of Feuerbach or Altizer. But it is immensely difficult to effect this transposition without suspecting that you are just formulating a reason you would like (rationalizing, or wishful thinking) so that permanency may nevertheless be asserted. For everything is against permanency: the very nature of time is that it passes; *panta rei* as Heraclitus said.

Nothing is worthwhile but man, and ultimately even man in himself is not worthwhile. As a Christian I am rather pessimistic about human nature in itself. You remember Chesterton's story of the criminal who disguised himself as a priest and gave himself away to Father Brown by saying man was good.

Faith arises in the human situation and involves dealing with men in faith. But it is not simply faith in men.

Transcendence is the point to concentrate on. That is, God as holy. But then the danger is that we lose touch with God as present in the world. So we must understand transcendence as this-worldly transcendence.

The question is: How do we understand this division between God and the world: as an abyss, a cleft impassable? or as a division which has been healed? If we really believe in the healing, or reconciliation, between God and man in Christ, as something which is a *novum*—something entirely new and unique and permanent—then we must be prepared to think everything new, including the way in which God is. This is the inwardness and the pathos of the death-of-God theologians, who do see, and rightly, that God is renewed as well as man by the Christ-event; he is drawn into history in such a total way that neither history nor God himself can ever be the same again. 'Only the suffering God can help.'[1] We must be prepared to take on ourselves the risk of patripassian ideas. Must we also understand God's self-emptying in Christ as the end of the old régime of God as plain Lord?

I have to assert God's transcendence *and* his presence: or, his presence in absence, his being in the world without being a phenomenon in the world. But he is present in a veiled way.

Beside the objectivity of inert objects in the world there is another kind of objectivity—that which is available in the relation of mutual apprehension in the 'realm' of the 'between'.

The question in what way the other makes himself available, i.e. apprehensible, to me is determined in its form by the way in which I am able to apprehend him. But the content of this mutual apprehension is not determined by either of us in isolation. But it cannot be said either simply to be lying there inert—an object in the sense of a thing which has its real existence outside of the mutual apprehension.

This is not a retreat into personal subjectivism.

To identify that in which faith believes and hopes with subjective freedom or responsibility or trust, no matter how radically interpreted, would be as great a mistake as to identify it as some kind of object, however ultimate.

Phenomenologists like Husserl derive the original nature of encounter from subjective empathy. Sociologists, like Buber, regard the 'Thou' as immediately given.

[1] D. Bonhoeffer, *Letters and Papers from Prison*, SCM Press, 1967, p. 197.

I myself would say that we begin neither with 'I' and the other 'I', but with the situation of Spirit in which 'Thou' and 'I' are interwoven.

To elucidate this there is a need for a new natural theology which is empirical, historical, positivist ('He that hath seen me hath seen the Father'), grounded in the Word. But this natural theology must at the same time be *fides quaerens intellectum*. In other words, there can be no God-talk without faith. Faith has the primacy and is active before, during and after all 'natural' theology. Everything is given, is of grace. The Word as a speech-event—i.e. as the reality of history summoning man to be himself—is the only reality. (How to adjust this conviction to the exigencies of the tradition is a problem of historical criticism. It is not the basic problem. The basic problem is how to help others to endure life.)

Such a new natural theology will involve first of all a theological rejection. What is rejected is a certain conceptuality or framework of thought. It is commonly said that this is primarily a rejection of any metaphysics, and by this is meant either the discarding of the frame of thought inherited from mediaeval scholasticism, of a natural and a supernatural order, etc.; or the discarding of traditional natural theology as a necessary preliminary stage to the acceptance of divinely revealed truths.

In place of these rejected alternatives a great many candidates rush in to fill the vacuum in thought thus created. Before we examine any of them, and before we go on to propose our own way out of the theological impasse, it should, I think, be said that whatever is done must be done by way of rational analysis; by way, that is, of understanding the phenomena of faith. This means in effect that there can be no theology that is not in some sense philosophical. That is, it is not merely the explication of traditional doctrines; but it is the explication of the phenomena of faith.

The bland conviction that the old traditions are *as such* normative must be rejected. But as soon as faith seeks an understanding of itself, the whole gamut of theological tradition is bound to enter in again, but in a new way.

I wish therefore to draw together my reflections in terms of a few categorical remarks. (I hardly dare to give them the exalted name of theses.)

1. I cannot subscribe to any conception of God's being-for-himself as the leading or dominating conception for Christian faith. But on the other hand this does not mean that I subscribe to the simple conception of God's total implication in the creative processes of history. Nor can I, with Ogden, attempt to rescue God from total implication in the creative processes of history by asserting an abstract principle for God as the absolute ground of all relatedness. Nor can I, with Karl Barth, simply push through to the conception of God's sovereign freedom as active and real within his intra-trinitarian relationships. The grandeur of this construction of Barth's must not blind us to the violence which is done here, by a speculative postulation, to the very sources of that speculation —namely, to the historical events which constitute the material for the message concerning Christ.

2. We face here a real antinomy. We are here really

up against the boundary of human possibility. We cannot talk about God directly. And if we talk, as I believe we can and must do, about God indirectly, in terms of his historical transformations (*Wandlungen*), then we are once more in danger of assimilating God either to our own self-understanding or, more generally, to the historical process. The latter view is attractive (as for instance Thomas Altizer has found and shown). But it has one flaw, and it is fatal: it means that God is at the end, but not at the beginning. He becomes sheer temporality.

3. But you may reply: why not? If we discard the metaphysical arguments and the objectifying method, what have we left but the sheer temporality of history? Moreover, can we not regard this tendency—namely the affirmation of sheer temporality—as implicit in the belief in the Incarnation? One must certainly admit that the most tempting of all the traditional heresies today is that of patripassianism, namely, the belief that the Father also suffers. D. Bonhoeffer is clearly tempted in his talk of a suffering God to cut the metaphysical knot, and to reduce Christianity to a view of life which is simply the view from the cross of Christ, so to speak. I do not wish to adduce Bonhoeffer, however, as an example of one who has succumbed to this temptation—he is far too complex a figure for this simple accusation. But the temptation is there, precisely because there can be no doubt that the suffering Christ in history is an absolutely central reality for our grasp of, for our being grasped by, the love which can introduce into our historical situation a new element, namely, the overcoming of the old world of sin

and death, and the offering of a real hope in and through and for this world, in the name of a triumphant suffering, i.e. in the name of the triumphant Sufferer. And any view of the reality of Christ's love which ignores the reality of his triumph cannot, it seems to me, be any more than a heroic gesture of defiance in face of a bleak and meaning-less world. So we cannot really rest in the simple and activist affirmation of Christ as the man for others, and not even as the suffering man for others. But as soon as we seek to say more, what can we say? We speak of him as the resurrection and the life, or as the exalted Lord: but are we in this terminology really getting beyond a mythological assertion, in which we are just saying something about our own attitudes to life?

4. I still think that there is a third alternative, which is neither that of an objectifying metaphysic nor that of an immanentist process view of history. And this third alternative arises out of a radical assessment of what is implied in the historicity of man. I have already indicated that this historicity is not fully self-explanatory. In every historical encounter there is a residue or an overplus of mystery. Man is not simply a doer, he is primarily a receiver. He receives the reality which is possible in each encounter. From whence does he receive it? He receives it from the other: more precisely, by way of the other: in truth he receives the reality from the realm that lies between him and the other. This reality is neither himself nor the other: but in its entirety it lies between the two. There is a hinterland here which cannot be explicated. I meet the other: we enter into our common reality. We

neither acquire the other, nor do we possess the reality. We participate in it.

This participation means that we are permitted to point to what summons us, addresses us. Even in the so-called straightforward relationships which we may have with our friends and our companions in work, even with those we know and love best, we are aware that we are simply permitted to participate in a common situation. The fulness of the making-present of this participation does not mean that we comprehend the other: but it means that in facing the other we glimpse a mystery.

Must we then after all be content to say that it is a mystery of *being*, or of *eternity*? The traditional theology clings to the concept of being. Even Martin Buber, who has done so much to put the eminently human relation of I and Thou into the forefront of our consciousness, is ready to speak of the eternal: 'in each Thou we address the eternal Thou':[1] in each genuinely relational event there is a breath of the eternal Thou.

I do not think we can relinquish the insights that have been so hardly gained through the new modern concern with historicity. At the risk of being too primitive and altogether too exposed to traditional critiques, I venture to suggest the way along which a viable theology is possible with full recognition of the insights of a genuine secularity.

First, theology must indeed learn to be more modest. Talk of the historicity of man does not mean that we can talk of a meaning to history as a whole. But it simply

[1] *I and Thou*, T. and T. Clark, Edinburgh, 1937, p. 101.

means that we can, and must, talk out of our own historical experience, and nothing else. (Of course this means talking of our received tradition as well; but always in constant criticism of it.) Theology, in a word, must learn when to be silent.

But secondly, we may really talk of God as involved in our historicity. This does not lead to a general view of the so-called 'creative processes' of history: but it leads us to the recognition of the otherness, and behind the otherness that 'something else'—what I have already described as the reality of the spirit.

Thirdly, this recognition of otherness excludes any possibility of our simply identifying God with human historicity. Even in the faith that God has given himself wholly in Christ into history, there is still a sense in which that giving is not complete. This is expressed mythologically in the expectation of the second coming of Christ, and it is expressed existentially by our acknowledgment that our faith is a prolepsis, an anticipation, of the end. But the end is not yet. What we recognize here, in the otherness of God, is not that God is swallowed up in human history, but that human history ends in God.

Fourthly, we therefore cannot speak of completion. From our human standpoint neither the beginning nor the end can be directly apprehended: both beginning and end are matters of faith.

Fifthly, the denial by faith that God is either a state of being or a continuing self-creation carries with it the positive affirmation that he must be regarded as the continual self-realization of what he is. This self-realization of what he is cannot however be identified with a being-of-God, whether as 'Being' (*Sein*) or 'being there' (*Dasein*) or 'being to hand' (*Vorhandensein*). God is for faith not a static entity or the ground of being. He is not simply the historical *Dasein* of Jesus. And he is all the less simply at our disposal as an object in the world.

Primarily, faith does not say 'I believe that', but 'I believe in'. Of course this does not exclude both *notitia* and *assensus*, but these are secondary. There is no *sacrificum intellectus* called for; on the contrary, the powers of the intellect are called into play all along the line. For faith faces the demand of God as the ultimate partner, not as an object but as the one who happens to me.

Sixthly, when categories of being, and simple identification with the processes of history, are alike excluded as inadequate ways of talking about God, does this mean that we are left with mere silence? In one sense, yes: for here we face the limits of human possibility. And in a deep sense, therefore, it seems to me that we must learn again what it means to say that God is *nihil*. By this *nihil* I do not mean a mere void or vacuum: but therewith I express the limit. God is beyond the limit. Is he then simply ineffable? By no means: but out of the *Ungrund*—the unfathomable depth—of this beyond-the-limit, which I indicate with the word *nihil*, there comes what we do know, and believe, and can talk about, namely, God for us in his historical being in Christ. We cannot know or believe or talk about anything else when we try to speak of God. We can guard our talk of God from *simple* temporality by recognizing in a contrapuntal way the unfathomable depths of his reality for which our only words are negatives, and this supreme negative, *nihil*. But this does not reduce or eliminate God's temporality, or his historicity: on the contrary, we are able to affirm that in God's self-realization in every Now he is himself: that is, his continual self-realization is at the same time his remaining constantly himself. And we face an antinomy for our thought here which cannot be resolved by recourse to either categories of being or to a self-evident and self-explanatory historical process.

Lastly, one thing more must be said: the self-realization of God in history can be most illuminatingly expressed under the aspect of personal being. This is an analogy from human personal being, but it is a real analogy. Even the human person, in its deficiency and incompleteness, can be recognized as being on the one hand thoroughly temporal and historical and on the other hand identical with itself. The deficiency and incompleteness of human personal being consist in the fact that it is always on the way, it receives itself as a possibility, which has to be realized ever anew in decision, whereas God's personal reality is a constant, constantly happening, self-tealization.

The thorough historicity of God, therefore, does not mean that he is reduced to simple human categories. Rather, it means that through the human historical understanding available to us, and through the self-understanding which is disclosed to us by the kerygma concerning Christ, we are able to recognize that *we* are not yet what we can be. God is entirely what he can be:

that is, we know and acknowledge him as the one who in being for us in history is at the same time entirely and fully personal. First we have a glimpse of what person means, when we are given our chance by the historical disclosures and movements of God through history: we recognize simultaneously that we are not what we can become and that God is entirely what he can be.

God is therefore a name that we may use, and must use, in fear and trembling, as the one who is ineffable, yet gives himself a 'local habitation and a name', in his movements and transformations through history.

Christian faith must constantly look for a form to express this apprehension. It is an apprehension, not a comprehension. But Christian faith cannot go beyond itself for categories to express this apprehension. This is what I have tried throughout these lectures to do: namely, to express faith's concern in terms of insights of knowledge which are derived from faith itself. And we must always test these insights of knowledge against the actual historical demands of faith. In its greatest moments I believe that Christian faith has always been impelled by the conviction that the less encumbrances it has the better. It has again and again been accused of being too spare and sparse: it has always had to undertake immense reduction of its own baggage. This is the meaning of *ecclesia semper reformanda*. I believe that such a time is upon us again. Everything turns today on the one decision, the one risk, the staking your life on the inexpressible reality of God who is entirely historical, that is, entirely for man, and also entirely himself. But that God is entirely himself is not the same as entirely-for-himself. We know God by faith in what he does to us. More we do not know.

'Beloved, we are God's children now; it does not yet appear what we shall be, but we know that when he appears we shall be like him, for we shall see him as he is.' (I John 3: 2.)

As he is: this we shall see in the indescribable end, not the collapse of history, not the loss of time and significance, not the static 'isness' of an indifferent principle, but the endless fulfilment in an endless movement of reciprocity which we already glimpse and see as in a mirror, darkly.

List of Books

ALTIZER, J. J. *The Gospel of Christian Atheism*, 1966, Philadelphia

BAELZ, P. *Christian Theology and Metaphysics*, 1967, London

BAILLIE, J. *Our Knowledge of God*, 1939, London

BARTH, K. *Church Dogmatics*, 1957-1961, Edinburgh

BONHOEFFER, D. *Letters and Papers from Prison*, 1967, London

BRAUN, H. 'Die Problematik einer Theologie des Neuen Testaments',
   in *Zeitschrift für Theologie und Kirche*, Beiheft 2 September 1961

BRUNNER, E. *Revelation and Reason*, 1947, London

BUBER, M. *The Eclipse of God*, 1953, London
   I and Thou, 1937, Edinburgh
   Kingship of God, 1967, London

BULTMANN, R. *Das Evangelium des Johannes*, 1950, Göttingen

BUREN, P. VAN, *The Secular Meaning of the Gospel*, 1963, London

BURKE, T. P. ed. *The Word in History*, 1968, London

CASPER, B. *Das dialogische Denken*, 1967, Freiburg

DORNER, I. *System der christlichen Glaubenslehre*, 1886

EBELING, G. *The Word of God and Tradition*, 1968, London

EBNER, F. *Das Wort und die geistigen Realitäten*, 1952, Vienna
   Gesammelte Schriften, 1954, Vienna

EICHRODT, W. *Theology of the New Testament*, 1961, London

GEERING, L. *God in the New World*, 1968, London

GLATZER, N. *Franz Rosenzweig, His Life and Thought*, 1953, New York

GOLLWITZER, H. *The Existence of God*, 1965, London

HATCH, E. *The Influence of Greek Ideas and Usages upon the Christian
   Church*, 1890, London

HEIDEGGER, M. *Introduction to Metaphysics*, tr. R. Manheim, 1959,
   London

JÜNGEL, E. *Gottes Sein ist im Werden*, 1965, Tübingen

KÄSEMANN, E. *Der Ruf der Freiheit*, 1968, Tübingen

KÖRNER, J. 'Die transzendente Wirklichkeit Gottes', in *Zeitschrift für Theologie und Kirche*, December 1966

LEWIS, H. D. *Philosophy of Religion*, 1965, London

MACQUARRIE, J. ed. *A Dictionary of Christian Ethics*, 1967, London (essay by R. Lee, 'Ethical Problems of Contemporary Society')

MACQUARRIE, J. *Principles of Christian Theology*, 1967, London
Studies in Christian Existentialism, 1966, London

MARSCH, W. D. *Die Gegenwart Christi*, 1965, Munich

MASCALL, E. *He Who Is*, 1943, London

METZ, J. B. 'The Church and the World', in *The Word in History*, edited by T. P. Burke, 1968, London

MICHALSON, C. *Worldly Theology*, 1967, New York

MOLTMANN, J. *Theology of Hope*, 1967, London

NADLER, J. ed. *Sämtliche Werke von J. G. Hamann*, 1951, Vienna

NIEBUHR, R. *The Meaning of Revelation*, 1946, New York

OGDEN, S. *The Reality of God*, 1967, London

PRENTER, R. 'Bonhoeffer and Barth's Positivism Revelation', in *World Come of Age*, edited by R. Gregor Smith, 1967, London

RAD, G. von, *Old Testament Theology*, 1962, Edinburgh
Religion in Geschichte und Gegenwart (2nd Edition), 1927-1932, Tübingen

RAHNER, K. *Nature and Grace*, 1963, London
Theological Investigations, 1961, London
'Theology and Anthropology', in *The Word in History*, edited by T. P. Burke, 1968, London

ROBINSON, J. A. T. *Honest to God*, 1957 London

ROSENZWEIG, F. *Stern der Erlösung*, 1954, Heidelberg

SCHILLEBEECKX, E. 'Faith and Self-Understanding', in *The Word in History*, edited by T. P. Burke, 1968, London

SMITH, R. GREGOR, *J. G. Hamann, A Study in Christian Existence*, 1960, London
Secular Christianity, 1966, London
The Free Man, 1969, London
The Last Years, Journals by Søren Kierkegaard, 1965, London
The New Man, 1956, London

THEUNISSEN, M. 'Bubers negative Ontologie des Zwischen', in
  Philosophisches Jahrbuch, Vol. 71, Pt. 2, 1964, Munich
            Der Andere, 1965, Berlin
TILLICH, P. *Biblical Religion and the Search for Ultimate Reality*, 1955,
  London
  Systematic Theology, 1953, London
WITTGENSTEIN, L. *Philosophical Investigations*, 1958, Oxford

Index